Advance praise for *The 9 Faces of HR*

"Delivered in the fresh, street-savvy voice of prolific blogger and HR change agent Kris Dunn, *9 Faces* is a glorious, in-your-face exposé of the profiles for success or failure in our HR profession. *9 Faces* inspires, amuses, even offends at times, but ultimately it equips you with an informed awareness for maximum success, even the most challenging corporate environments."
—Doug Dean, CCP, Chief Human Resource Officer, Children's of Alabama

"Like any great artist of our time, Dunn is a master of his medium, effortlessly weaving pop culture and wit to breathe life into a daunting topic with an approachable framework to for HR pros to maximize influence — and their careers. Two enthusiastic thumbs up!"
—Holland Dombeck McCue, Head of Employer Brand, Delta Air Lines

"Insightful, refreshing, motivating and entertaining! I didn't put *The 9 Faces of HR* down until I read every single page. It's like a walk backwards through your career with a spotlight on the good, bad and ugly. I laughed, blushed and almost cried. It doesn't matter which stage of your career you are in or which of the 9 faces of HR resonates with you, you will emerge from this book with innovative ideas to take you, your team and your organization to the next level."
—Allison Cox, SVP Talent Management & Leadership Development, Simmons Bank

"Written in the spirit of empowering our profession, *9 Faces* in the most entertaining ways, *The 9 Faces of HR* forces HR to turn the mirror on *ourselves* (scary, I know) and identify who we are now, which "HR Face" we aspire to be, and what skills will make all HR pros viable and valued in the modern workforce."
—Dawn Burke, Career VP of HR, Founder of DawnBurkeHR

"If you want to change the trajectory of your career, the trajectory of the HR profession and the trajectory of the business you support—this book is written for you."
—Ed Baldwin, HR Director (People and Culture), Mikron

"This book will encourage, embolden and cause immense self-reflection on career choices and the purpose of HR in the next chapter of work."
—Kathy Rapp, Managing Partner, hrQ

"Kris Dunn is a true innovator in the talent space and I highly recommend *The 9 Faces of HR* for anyone looking to build a career or HR function that thinks differently and is valued by the C-level."
—Scott Stone, Principal, Butler Snow Advisory, Career CFO/COO

"*The 9 Faces of HR* is an exercise in self-examination for the HR professional and no matter where you are in your professional journey, you will benefit from this book."

—John Whitaker SHRM-SCP, Vice President Talent Acquisition, DentalOne Partners

"I started my HR career as one of Dunn's Assassin's, I like to think of myself now as The Natural, but I'm probably more of a Mentor on my best days. Reading *The 9 Faces of HR*, I felt a little like Lauren Hill, as Dunn was strumming my pain with his fingers, singing my life with his words, and telling my whole life in HR with this book. He definitely was killing me softly, in the best of ways!"

—Tim Sackett, President, HRU Technical, and author of *The Talent Fix*

THE 9 FACES OF HR

A Disruptor's Guide to Mastering Innovation
and Driving Real Change

THE 9 FACES OF HR

A Disruptor's Guide to Mastering Innovation and Driving Real Change

Kris Dunn

A playbook for empowering your HR career
and transforming the world's greatest profession

Society for Human Resource Management
Alexandria, Virginia www.shrm.org
Society for Human Resource Management, India
Mumbai, India www.shrmindia.org
Society for Human Resource Management
Haidian District Beijing, China www.shrm.org/cn
Society for Human Resource Management, Middle East and Africa Office
Dubai, United Arab Emirates www.shrm.org/pages/mena.aspx

This publication is designed to provide accurate and authoritative information regarding the subject matter covered. It is sold with the understanding that neither the publisher nor the author is engaged in rendering legal or other professional service. If legal advice or other expert assistance is required, the services of a competent, licensed professional should be sought. The federal and state laws discussed in this book are subject to frequent revision and interpretation by amendments or judicial revisions that may significantly affect employer or employee rights and obligations. Readers are encouraged to seek legal counsel regarding specific policies and practices in their organizations.

This book is published by the Society for Human Resource Management (SHRM). The interpretations, conclusions, and recommendations in this book are those of the author and do not necessarily represent those of the publisher.

SHRM, the Society for Human Resource Management, creates better workplaces where employers and employees thrive together. As the voice of all things work, workers and the workplace, SHRM is the foremost expert, convener and thought leader on issues impacting today's evolving workplaces. With 300,000+ HR and business executive members in 165 countries, SHRM impacts the lives of more than 115 million workers and families globally. Learn more at SHRM .org and on Twitter @SHRM.

Library of Congress Cataloging-in-Publication Data
Names: Dunn, Kris, author.
Title: The 9 faces of HR : discovering HR disruptors that add value, drive change, and champion innovation / Kris Dunn. Other titles: Nine faces of HR
Description: First edition. | Alexandria, VA : Society for Human Resource Management, [2019] | Includes bibliographical references and index.
Identifiers: LCCN 2019012952 (print) | LCCN 2019015391 (ebook) | ISBN 9781586445744 (PDF) | ISBN 9781586445768 (ePUB) | ISBN 9781586445775 (Mobi) | ISBN 9781586445737 (pbk. : alk. paper)
Subjects: LCSH: Personnel management.
Classification: LCC HF5549 (ebook) | LCC HF5549 .D864 2019 (print) | DDC 658.3--dc23

Printed in the United States of America   FIRST EDITION

PB Printing   10 9 8 7 6 5 4 3 2 1   SKU: 61.19301

Dedication

For my family (spousal FTE Angela, 2.4 FTE dependents Drew and Brady and a dysfunctional cat named Dorito), which is predictably nuclear while also following the arc of an underappreciated Netflix sitcom—thanks for the love, drama, support, and laughs.

For my parents, who taught me the value of waking up every day and competing at work, and also kept the house stacked with magazines that influenced me to write and have a point of view. RIP Kent and Deanna Dunn, I miss you.

For my HR brethren at all levels reading this hot take on your future prospects—shine on you crazy diamonds. I believe in you even when you don't. Create something new this month even if it pisses someone off.

Contents

List of Figures ix

Foreword xi

Preface xiii

Acknowledgments xv

1   Meet Jenn, VP of HR at GridLoad 1

2   Absolutely No One Grows Up Dreaming of a Career in HR. 5

3   My Life with the Crazy People Who Hate HR. 13

     Bonus: A Special Crazy Boss Story from KD's Diary. 21

4   HR Stereotypes and the Evolution of HR Saying "Yes" 25

     Bonus: "God's Plan" from Drake Is Telling You How to Do HR 33

5   HR's Big Innovation Problem 37

     Bonus: Jedi Mind Tricks from Salesforce.com
     "Equality Matters as Much as Diversity". 43

6   How the 9 Face of HR Model Works 49

7   The Great BS Artists Who Gave Us the 9-Box Grid
     and Performance vs. Potential. 55

8   HR Nerd Alert: The Four Factors that Drive the Ability to Innovate,
     Add Value, and Drive Change in HR 65

9   Professional Tourette's Is Dangerous (Cognitive Skills). 69

     Bonus: Revenue per Employee and the Emerging Title of "HR
     Capologist". 75

10   Give Me What I Want or I'll Ruin Your Career (Assertiveness). 79

     Bonus: He's a Good Guy, Except for the Jihad 85

11   Take this OPS Manual and Shove It (Rules Orientation) 89

     Bonus: How Elon Musk Decided if His Assistant Needed a Raise 95

12   May I Show You My Signed Picture of Dale Carnegie?
     (Detail Orientation). 101

13   Let's Do This: A Tour of the 9 Faces of HR. 107

14   The Natural 111

       Bonus: We're All Working for the Same Boss, Aren't We? 119

15   The Mentor 121

       Bonus: Quiz—How to Tell If You'll Be Running HR
       at a Great Company in the Next Ten Years. 129

16   The Judge 133

       Bonus: Lessons from Uber: Sometimes Your HR Job Changes 143

17   The Assassin 149

       Bonus: HR Metrics: Stop Measuring You and Start Measuring Them . . 157

18   The Fixer 161

       Bonus: The Five Biggest Lies In HR. 169

19   The Cop 173

20   The Rookie. 181

       Bonus: Does HR Certification or an MBA Make Me
       More Desirable in HR?. 189

21   The Clerk 193

22   The Machine 201

       Bonus: A.I.'s "Gaydar" Is Better Than Yours, But That's Probably
       Going to Go Horribly Wrong 209

23   Your Future Boss Thinks You Suck! 213

24   Staying Alive: Using The 9 Faces of HR to Protect and Build
       your Career 221

25   Build It and They Will Come: Using the 9 Faces of HR
       as a CHRO/VP of HR 231

26   C-Level Notes: Using The 9 Faces of HR Model to Find
       and Select a CHRO/VP of HR 239

27   Career Mobility Inside The 9 Faces of HR Model 245

28   Closing Time 251

Index   253

About the Author   259

Other SHRM Books   261

Books Approved for SHRM Recertification Credits   263

List of Figures

Figure 6.1.   The 9 Faces of HR Model   50

Figure 7.1.   McKinsey's 9-Box Grid   57

Figure 7.2.   The Performance vs Potential Grid   59

Figure 8.1.   First Look Scorecard   66

Figure 14.1.   Roger, the Natural   111

Figure 14.2.   Scorecard for the Natural   114

Figure 15.1.   Jill the Mentor   121

Figure 15.2.   Scorecard of the Mentor   126

Figure 16.1.   Andrea the Judge   133

Figure 16.2.   Scorecard for the Judge   137

Figure 17.1.   Chloe the Assassin   149

Figure 17.2.   Scorecard for the Assassin   151

Figure 18.1.   Jim the Fixer   161

Figure 18.2.   Scorecard for Fixer   166

Figure 19.1.   Alesha the Cop   173

Figure 19.2.   Scorecard for the Cop   177

Figure 20.1.   Veronica the Rookie   181

Figure 20.2.   Scorecard for the Rookie   186

Figure 21.2.   Scorecard for the Clerk   197

Figure 22.1.   Brenda the Machine   201

Figure 22.2.   Scorecard for the Machine   205

Figure 24.1.   Scorecard for KD   223

Figure 27.1.   Career Mobility   245

Figure 27.2.   Career Path   247

Foreword

If we're being completely honest with each other, I don't think I've ever given Kris Dunn proper credit for the impact he's had on me. To that end, for all that he's done for me, an acknowledgement is overdue. So, we'll call the foreword for this book just that—a thanks and an endorsement for the guy they call "KD".

Much like how I discovered KD's HR Capitalist blog 11 years ago, you'll pick up this book and just keep reading. That's what happens with KD and his words. You get sucked in. I finished my advanced copy of this book at the start of an international flight thinking it would be what I needed to pass out and sleep. (It's an HR book after all.) But instead, it kept me up and I read it cover to cover much to my annoyance given the jetlag ahead of me and much to my delight because... it's really good. And it reminded me of all of the reasons why KD is that good.

You can't help but to think as you read... oh my God, he's totally in my HR brain, and thinks about HR and all of its possibilities like I do. Or for me, how I aspire to. Which is refreshing, and hopeful that HR doesn't have to be the butt of all jokes. There will be moments where you could basically swap out the HR pro's name in some of the chapters for yours because the stories are all too familiar. And in later moments, it will be clarifying because you'll quickly see how something you had previously effed up should have been handled, and how you'll work to react in the future.

And that's the KD effect and this book in a nutshell.

More on the effect. You quickly become a fan boy/girl because somehow, KD will have made it (dare I say) entertaining and fun to learn. So, you'll become a better HR pro as a result. And for those of us who have been lucky enough to be a part of his orbit, ultimately you find yourself not just better but rather, performing at your best—which has happened multiple times over the years for me.

The first time, it was that he gave me a platform for my voice through a little 'ole blog now known as Fistful of Talent. KD helped me to rediscover what I loved—writing—and enabled me to get a whole lot better at it by giving me a shot at contributing first, and ultimately becoming the site's editor next. Not to mention, the side benefits of becoming more comfortable with having strong opinions, homing in on the idea of having a personal brand and the irreplaceable HR industry relationships I built as a result of my perch on that blog.

As it was actually happening though, I didn't even realize how he was nudging me and what I was gaining because of him. He's got an eye for talent that's better than anyone I've ever met and can see what we're capable of as individuals and a collective. He knows that we've all got something to offer—regardless of which face of HR you are today. He's got faith in what we're working with and that maybe, just maybe, with his nudge in the right direction, we will be on our way to becoming a better version of ourselves. The best version if you're lucky.

So please read on, enjoy it, and go do some good.

And now, back to the credit due to KD. While it always seems like I'm half-hearted with my thanks, Kris… know that I will always be grateful that you've long believed in me. Thanks for all of the assists over the years, even if my shots haven't always ended up as points on the board.

—Jessica Lee
VP, Brand Talent, Marriott International
Bethesda, Maryland

Preface

If I've learned one thing over twenty years as a manager, director, and VP of HR for big and small companies alike, it's that great HR *matters*. While HR has long been considered a backwater by the salty characters from other departments, we all encounter in our daily corporate lives great HR pros who have a way of making people stand up and take notice, often causing the following reaction: " *WTF?*"

When the non-believers curse, they don't curse because they find the HR pro in front of them non-credible. They curse because they didn't expect to be challenged. And that's the whole point— non-believers love bad HR. They love bad HR because it means they either do what they want as quickly as possible, or inaction and delays get blamed on someone else.

Great HR, on the other hand, is a revenue producer. No, I don't have the return on investment (ROI) study on that—stop reading now if you need that. I didn't need the stat sheet to know that Steph Curry was different or that Carrie Underwood was going to be the most successful American Idol contestant. Like great HR Pros, Steph and Carrie were just different. They had "it."

What is "it?" That's kind of what this whole book is about, my friends.

I wrote this book for you. If you're reading this book, you're probably an HR pro at the manager, director, or VP level with an interest in getting to or staying on top. You might also be a C-level looking for a path to hire a great HR leader after coming up short in previous searches. Either way, think of me as your personal agent. This book is about HR careers and what the world is looking for when it comes to great HR.

Your HR career moves pretty fast these days. If you don't stop and look around once in a while, you could miss it.

—KD

Acknowledgments

Props to HR legends Tim Sackett and Dawn Burke for always being willing to brainstorm ideas, only a portion of which made it to this book. The rest were left on the editing room floor, usually because they "were too much for the man."

Shout out to all my current and past writers at *Fistful of Talent*, most of whom exist on the right-hand side of the 9 Faces of HR. That's where many freaks and pirates exist on the grid.

Special thanks to Angela Dunn for early copy-editing as *The 9 Faces of HR* came to life. I'll buy you a new red pen to replace the one that ran out of ink.

1

Meet Jenn, VP of HR at GridLoad

You were the first to say we were not okay.
—*Life Starts Now* by Three Days Grace

T uesdays suck.
The relative merits of Tuesday domineered the mind of Jennifer Gottlieb as she looked through the back window of the Mercedes GLS in front of her in standstill traffic. Interstate 75 northwest of Atlanta proper had a growing reputation as a trap for commuters, intensified by the flight of the Atlanta Braves from downtown to the junction of I–75 and I–285—and the construction that followed.

Tuesdays, thought Jenn (no one called her Jennifer except her mom and one of her HR coordinators who was as old as her mom), were sneaky in their level of suck. Everyone knows that Mondays are generally awful; Wednesdays have the reputation as hump day; and Thursdays and Fridays are close enough to the weekend to put you at ease. Tuesdays though? Sneaky in their level of despair.

Jenn muttered "wealthy old woman car" under her breath as she watched the redhead in front of her put on makeup as they creeped along at five mph. Her younger brother, now a senior at Georgia Tech, loved to typecast people by their cars. He used the phrase to describe their aunt who also drove the GLS. Jenn felt appropriately placed as a 34-year old in her BMW.

The commute wasn't always this bad. She used to live inside the perimeter of Atlanta, but her husband convinced her to make the full outside the perimeter move to the suburbs five years ago when they had both been promoted. Woodstock is where they ended up, which Jenn's friends referred to as BFE. It seemed simple enough—time to start a family, and the commute down to the Windy Hill area of 75/285 wasn't bad. Then the Braves moved from the city and all hell broke loose. The family had been put on hold when a subsequent promotion for her husband put him on the road four days a week.

"Ed was here ten minutes ago looking for you."

Damn. Of course, he was. She thanked Denise, one of her HR coordinators who had been with her for the past five years and started walking down the hall to Ed's office. Ed was the CEO at GridLoad, brought in by the private equity firm that took control of the company eight months ago.

As she walked, Jenn thought about the current leadership team (LT). In the eight months Ed had been CEO, he had replaced three of eight LT members, a group in which Jenn served as the VP of HR. The "survivors"—as the remaining five liked to call themselves—served as a support group for each other. Most of them considered Ed to be a complete prick. Jenn was careful never to be heard framing Ed in such terms as the HR leader, but she couldn't disagree.

"Where are we with the openings in software development?" Ed never wasted time on pleasantries. As soon as Jenn was physically in his office, the questions usually started before she sat down. Today's topic was a familiar one—the lag time in recruiting the software developers who were the lifeblood of product development at GridLoad.

Jenn responded to Ed, citing new postings that had been purchased, contingency recruiters who were working on the openings, and a call for referrals her department had made across the company.

Ed seemed less than impressed and asked her to update Rich, the VP of software development, on the status. Sensing the meeting was over by Ed's body language, Jenn rose to walk back to her

office and said, "See you at the leadership team update at 1 p.m."
Ed mumbled "Yep" as he started to scan his email.

Jenn didn't realize it as she walked down the hall, but she was already dead.

Her career was over at GridLoad. She just didn't know it yet.

2

Absolutely No One Grows Up Dreaming of a Career in HR

Personnel? That's for a**holes!
—Harry Callahan (Clint Eastwood) upon discovering
he was being reassigned in *Dirty Harry* (1976)

Did Jenn grow up dreaming of a career in HR? Probably not. Raise your hand if you grew up dreaming of a career in HR. It's okay, I'll wait.

No one? Of course not. The dirty little secret of HR is that most of us didn't have a master plan to end up managing people's functions and maximizing human capital return on investment (ROI) inside the modern workplace. We grew up with bigger dreams, which is cool because no one grows up dreaming of being a director of account management, a financial analyst, or a marketing manager, either.

Those dreams all suck when you're sixteen.

Instead, the teenage version of ourselves dreamed of being a movie star, a recording artist, or a professional athlete. The freaks among us were entrepreneurial from the time they were five and likely knew they'd own their own business. The rest of us float, usually until we pick a major in college, at which time our career paths and ambitions solidify.

But the choice of HR as a career path happens later than most on average. For all the undergraduate programs in HR, the ubiquitous nature of the Society for Human Resources Management (SHRM) and the increasing importance of the human capital function, many meaningful HR pros don't solidify a path into HR until they're in the workforce doing other things.

Translation: Many HR pros will tell you they "fell" into HR.

Falling into HR Is the Norm, Not the Exception

Here's a non-comprehensive list of other things people fall into:

»   Love
»   Addiction
»   A bad relationship
»   Lucky circumstances in life
»   Debt
»   Religious cults
ˋ   A habit of eating a pint of mint chocolate chip ice cream at 9 PM nightly.

That list tells you that falling into things can be a blessing and a curse—it's all relative to the outcome. From my experience talking to the talented high performers who make up the world of HR, here's some common ways people fall into HR without a real plan to enter the function that's loved and hated by so many:

»   **I started from the bottom, now I'm here.** You are a bootstrapper! Right out of college, these people took entry level roles in our company, usually doing transactions as an HR coordinator, payroll specialist, or similar role. They enjoyed the function and, in many cases, rose to run the whole damn thing. HR pros who find themselves entering the function in this manner have the greatest opportunity for career path growth in HR with small and medium-sized businesses.

»   **I'm a people person. I am good with the damn people.** These HR pros were generally present in a company and got identified as someone who was "good with people," and subsequently flipped into the HR function from another department. When looking at this group, "good with people" is a broad designation that can mean they are extroverted, good listeners, or are willing to take large amounts of bulls*** and abuse without exploding. It can also mean they have skills in actually solving other people's problems and maximizing others' performance inside the organization. While the latter designation is preferred, being labeled as "good with people" is rarely that deep.

» **I'm a corporate paratrooper or a High Potential Employee (HIPO)—I got dropped into the function on an interim basis and never left.** Big companies have rotational programs for HIPOs as part of succession strategies, and HR is generally part of that rotation. In some cases, HIPOs are rotated into HR and end up loving it and being highly effective. They either never leave or come back to HR after their rotations are complete. In other circumstances, high performers are parachuted into HR on an interim basis to put out a burning dumpster fire and find their perfect match and stay for the good times.

» **A friend or mentor who had an opening looked at you and said, "WTF?"** From time to time, the path into HR is based on friendship, with a high performing HR leader developing mentoring relationships with young professionals outside the organization and bringing them in when they have the opportunity. This generally involves the HR leader in question selling the non-HR talent on the fact that a career in HR is a good thing. The protégé decides to trust the HR mentor, takes the job, and the rest, as they say, is history.

» **I was good at a specialty related to HR and ended up running the whole HR show.** Feeder groups for HR include some specialties that are considered a distant or related cousin to the HR function—like training or recruiting. This close proximity to the HR function provides a natural exposure and transition point to HR for the professionals in those functions with the chops to handle the chaos that awaits them in the big show.

» **I failed in another job at our company, and they moved me into HR so they didn't have to fire me.** I didn't want to include this one, but no rundown of all the ways people fall into a HR career would be complete without it. HR has a reputation in some company cultures as a backwater, a way station for average people doing average things. This leads to the perception that good people struggling in other areas can be dumped into HR. This seems to be decreasing in frequency, but it's a historic reality of our lives together in HR.

You can probably add to the list of ways that people fall into HR. If you're an HR pro who has an HR degree and has always possessed the clarity that comes with knowing you'd be in HR since you were twelve, Godspeed to you. Don't screw up your dream.

There Are Eight Million Stories in the Naked City

But it's rarely that clean for the rest of us. Consider the story of how I (Kris Dunn, aka "KD") fell into HR. It's a doozy:

1. **I graduated from Northeast Missouri State (now Truman State) and started a career as a young Division I college basketball coach at UAB** (University of Alabama–Birmingham), because that's how great HR is born, right? LOL.

2. **As a coaching staff member at a Division I program, I probably witnessed nine thousand conflicts with widely accepted people practices in corporate America,** even though I wasn't familiar with the terms "people practices," "corporate America," or "HR".

3. **After three years in coaching, I decided I was likely to be poor for a long time and exited the coaching game to go back to get my MBA** while working overnight in a wireless call center to pay the bills.

4. **While working overnight in the call center, a soon to be mentor named Marilyn Brooks (director of HR) figured out I had some potential in random post-shift interactions in the hallways and parking lot.** She decided to seek me out for a project evaluating staffing vendors as part of a request for proposal (RFP) process they were going through. I worked on the project overnight and delivered a lot more than was required. Mrs. Brooks was pleased.

5. **After getting my MBA, my wife and I relocated back home to Missouri (St. Louis area)** where she became a staff prosecutor, and I went to work doing market research for IBM Global.

6. **We went through one winter from hell, looked at each other and said, "what the hell are we doing?"** Even though we were from the Midwest, five years in the new South had thinned our blood, and we wanted to get back to the Southeast.

7. **With LinkedIn not even a glimmer in a venture capitalist's eye at the time, I started calling people I knew** (Marilyn Brooks among them), seeking career opportunities that would get me back to warm winters.

8. **Marilyn's words:** "I don't have anything in what you're doing now, but I do have a HR manager spot. Would you be interested in that? You used to be a coach and there's a lot of coaching in this role."

9. **I interviewed and got the job.** I was on my way in the world of HR.

Many of you are reading this and shaking your head. Some of you hate me for falling into this opportunity without paying my dues. Bottom line is this—I had a mentor of sorts, did good work to reinforce the mentor's belief in me, and the mentor ended up plugging in a non-traditional protégé into an opening on her HR team.

S**t like this happens all the time in HR. Film at 11.

Look Closely and Hollywood Shows
Us How People Fell into HR

There are only a few HR characters coming out of Hollywood. But all you have to do is look closely, and you can tell how they fell into the world of HR. Here are five that come to mind, and their match related to how they fell into our world of people, process, and corporate politics:

» **Toby Flenderson from *The Office*—**Poor Toby. We smile and cry as HR pros when we watch him fumble through his day. Quick to rely on policy and process and slow to confront anyone directly and aggressively, Toby without question fell into HR by taking a transactional role and finding a place where he could survive. You and I get to deal with the stereotype. Lucky us.

» **Mary Winetoss, the rules-obsessed head of human resources hell-bent on curtailing the hijinks of office workers planning to throw a wild holiday bash in the 2016 R-rated film *Office Christmas Party*—**Because she is a lesser known Hollywood HR character, you might be tricked based on her early reliance on policy that she's like Toby. That's an incorrect take, because her connection and problem solving with the leaders of her company clearly tells us she fell into the role based on being a "people person."

» **Dirty Harry in *The Enforcer* (1976)—**The iconic scene in this movie depicts Harry's boss announcing Harry has been demoted to "personnel," which clearly matches our earlier "don't fire them, move them to HR" path. Harry doesn't take the demotion well, pondering the move for two seconds before saying, "Personnel? That's for a**holes!" Thanks, Dirty Harry.

» **Pam Poovey from *Archer* (FX)—**Many of you don't know Archer, but your kids probably do. Archer is an adult animated sitcom created by Adam Reed for the cable network FX. It follows the exploits of a dysfunctional group of secret agents, with

Poovey being the group's director of HR. Ridiculed by her client group, but secretly capable of spy work with no training, Poovey clearly fell into HR by being dropped into our function at some point on an interim basis and finding a comfortable home there.

» **Ryan Bingham in *Up in The Air*** (2009)—Partial credit here since Bingham (played by George Clooney) is a specialist who lays people off for a living. Still, as you listen to Bingham wax poetic about travel program points and benefits and remain distant from the people he's firing, it's hard to imagine he's not an HIPO who parachuted into the world of HR, got comfortable with the perks, and never left.

My point to all of this? Most of us fell into HR. Some of the stories are funny, some are cautionary tales, and some reinforce stereotypes.

How you got here doesn't matter. To survive in a world of change, you're going to have to connect to the world around you and have more self-awareness of how you're perceived. That's what the rest of this book is about. Let's dig into what the people writing the checks want from HR and what that means for you.

3

My Life with the Crazy People Who Hate HR

They hate us cause they ain't us.
—Attributed to countless people with irrational confidence

I've been in HR for over twenty years. I'm somewhat of an expert on people who hate HR.

For the youngsters reading this book, I'm sorry. You're full of hope and energy and you're going to do great things. But I'm here to tell you there are people who will try to slap you in the face simply because you're an HR pro.

Those people suck. This chapter is about figuring out who they are and how to deal with them.

Identifying People Who Hate HR

Whether you're a HR leader of a *Fortune* 500 HR team or a solo practitioner in a company with one hundred employees, you've got people in your company who hate HR.

Hate might be a strong word. They hold your profession in contempt. They view you as a secretary with a policy manual.

No, on second thought, they hate you.

They hate you because they view you as one of several things based on their viewpoint:

» A no-talent hack
» A blocker impeding them from doing whatever they want to do
» Someone who doesn't know as much about people-related issues as they do
» The source of more work for them and six new passwords they must remember based on your commitment to "best in breed" HR technology solutions

Maybe you can solve that last one by running a workshop to show people how Chrome can automatically save passwords for future automated use, right?

Wrong. They won't attend your workshop because they loathe you. Let's cover the type of people who hate HR via the following list:

» **The Control Freak**—Sally's a control freak. She's a really smart person, has between ten and twenty years of experience in her non-HR functional areas, and has a hard time giving up control, which is code for the fact she can't collaborate beyond allowing her assistant to order lunch from Chipotle. She'll be damned if she's going to let you hone in on her hiring process for her next departmental hire.
» **The Power Broker**—The close cousin of the control freak, Rick's a power broker, which means he's learned multiple times in his career that getting HR involved in his business just slows him down. There are rules, policies, and various other distractions, and Rick just needs to execute. As a result of his experiences, Rick has learned that it's far better to beg for forgiveness than to ask you for permission. He has a smirk on the rare occasion he thinks of calling you, right before he tells his minions there's no need to reach out to HR.

» **The Victim of Bad HR**—Jean's an executive in your company. Her career started at a very conservative organization with a basic HR team that did payroll, fired people, and recruited via the post and pray model. Every two years, the HR function at her old company attempted to move upstream and it always failed, causing Jean to trust HR as much as her ex-husband.

» **The Reader of Best-Selling Business Books**—Bobby is a young director-level talent in your company. During his rise from the associate level, Bobby experienced two things—he didn't consider the HR team to be helpful or to be his peer, and he started reading best-selling business books like *The Five Dysfunctions of the Team*. He's all in on the management trends he's reading about and has asked some members of your team if they've read the books. When they say they haven't, it just solidifies Bobby's belief that he's got a better view on how to manage talent than your HR team.

Are any of these people's thoughts related to HR actually true? That's complicated. If you're reading this book and looking inward at the HR function, it's likely that you are part of the solution, not part of the problem. Unfortunately, most of you read the profiles and thought something along the lines of, "yeah, that's totally Margie."

Margie is someone you work(ed) with in HR. She's the person all of the HR haters love to point to.

Dammit, Margie—get your s**t together.

How the People Who Hate HR Will Stick It to You

The first thing you must realize about the people who hate HR is that it's never personal. If someone hates HR, those feelings were solidified long before you came on the scene.

There's a chance you're awesome. The downside of being awesome in HR is that you're expecting business leaders and the managers of people around you to see your talent. Most of them won't. That's why you need to be able to spot how HR haters are running around you to do whatever they want and, at times, perform at a lower level than they would have if they had included you.

Here are the behaviors to be on the lookout for as the people who hate HR attempt to avoid you and your team:

» **Make employment decisions without consulting you.** They just do it. Begging for forgiveness and thinking you're so weak that you can't check them. They're daring you to do something about it.

» **Give counsel to their direct reports about people issues without having them check in with you.** They're the expert, not you. You'll slow them down. They move fast. Rationalization: they run the business, you don't.

» **Use outside resources without giving you the chance to provide service.** Whether it's training, recruiting, or another service, when they have a need for service they don't even think about you—they call an outside expert.

» **Talk trash about you and your team to others not yet in the hating camp.** Business conversations happen everywhere in your company. The HR haters are always quick to scoff at your team's ability to handle things beyond payroll, which impacts your reputation in the organization.

» **Run their own HR-related sessions (think succession planning) without your help.** A favorite of the "Reader of Best-Selling Business Books" profile, HR haters with maximum confidence love to run their own HR processes within their departments and functions. They must be stopped.

» **Attack HR's credibility when confronted.** After dealing with assorted bulls*** from these haters, the strongest among you will be compelled to confront them. Don't expect them to be contrite; the first thing they'll do is go on the attack.

This book isn't about the haters of HR, but in order to understand how to maximize yourself from a career perspective, you have to identify and understand the haters to be able to deal with them.

That would be easy if it were just you. But most of you have an HR team, which increases the complexity of the situation to the level of SpaceX landing a reusable rocket on a barge in the Atlantic Ocean.

The Passive Behavior You Will See on Your Team Related to Dealing with HR Haters

If you're reading this book, you're either an HR alpha or would like to become an alpha. The same is not true for your team. One of the reasons I wrote a book on the 9 Faces of HR is because our profession is full of behavioral profiles that drive the way we respond to clients. You'll learn about the 9 Faces of HR soon. For now, tell me if you see yourself, or your team, in any of the following passive paths taken by people on your HR team as they deal with HR Haters:

» **HR is service oriented; therefore, we tell ourselves the customer is always right.** It's pure rationalization, of course. The customer of HR is not always right; we've just got a cross section of people who would rather not think about the alternatives.

» **HR fails to confront people doing bad things.** The alternative to the customer always being right, of course, is to first confront the general sense of lawlessness. It doesn't matter what *could* come next—if you're unwilling to confront, the next step never comes. And the craziness continues.

» **HR fails to negotiate a middle ground with HR haters.** HR is great at a lot of things. Negotiation is not one of those things. The solution is often as simple as confronting, then negotiating. More on this fun fact later.

» **HR fails to understand all the tools at their disposal to play offense with those who dare to question the function's**

credibility. Some HR leaders are political masters, Machiavellian in their daily craft. But others are unwilling to do what it takes to wrestle control of the organization. This book is, at times, about that political wrestling match.

Recognize any of these behaviors on your team? You've got great people on your team, but many of them are uncomfortable with activity that, at times, feels like confrontation.

As luck would have it, willingness to confront is the only consistent factor that converts an HR hater to a friend and colleague—or at least someone who respects the function.

Strategies for Dealing with People Who Hate HR

You'll see later in this book that the preferred strategies for dealing with the world around you depend on which of the 9 Faces of HR you identify with. That said, the strategies for dealing with people who hate HR are consistent, including the following must haves:

» **Playing Offense.** This is the preferred strategy because once you're in your organization for a year, you know who the haters are, right? Playing offense means you do things like reach out to them directly on any initiative, hold meetings with their boss (and them) to talk about your plans, and generally get in front of the hate. You're absolutely daring them to continue their hating ways by adding proactive leverage to your game.

» **Playing Defense.** This is clearly the backup strategy to playing offense. Even if there are only so many hours in the day, you're not going to think of everything. Haters will be active and play their game, so defense means you're going to have to play a big game of Whack-A-Mole.

» **Mastering Multiple Negotiation Tactics.** Whether you're playing offense or defense, the most effective tool for any HR leader in their arsenal is mastery of multiple negotiation tactics. When you read this, you automatically thought of buying a house or a car. That's one valuable negotiating method, but to really lean in to negotiation you'll have to learn three to four additional techniques, all designed to put the HR hater in a little box where their slippery ways don't cause you pain. More to come on this as we dig into the 9 Faces of HR.

The last strategy for dealing with people who don't respect the HR function is simple—Love the Game. Simply put, the workplace is a difficult place, and HR is one of the most complex functions due to its mix of science, subjectivity, and performance art. If you're going to survive and advance in the HR world, you're going to have to deal with those who don't want to hear what you have to say.

That's why I wrote this book. Regardless of your profile, there's a path for you to maximize yourself in the world of HR. You're good enough. You're smart enough. And gosh darn it, sometimes you need to stop worrying if people like you.

Bonus

A Special Crazy Boss Story from KD's Diary

It was Christmas Eve. Time for anticipation. Time for reflection. Time for an outrageous demand towards a candidate that could only occur from the bowels of corporate America and a boss with no respect for people—or for HR.

Gather around the tree kids, because it's story time, KD/HR Capitalist style. Bring me a Diet Mountain Dew while you're at it, because this eggnog sucks.

Everyone here? Good.

The year is 2002, and it's Christmas Eve. I had just become a VP of HR in corporate America, and got a new boss who, let's say, was a little intense. I found myself at home on Christmas Eve piddling with some work, etc. when my phone rang. I flexed my bicep (remember, phones were much bigger then), picked up the phone, and answered the call. It was my boss. Here's how the conversation went:

> **Capitalist (aka KD)**: Don, what's up?
>
> **Bossman/Executive Vice President (2B Line of business)**: Kris, glad I got you. I'm ready to make an offer to the director of finance candidate we like.
>
> **Capitalist**: Sweet. I'll call her today and let her know. Nice Christmas present.
>
> **Bossman**: Great. Just one little catch. I need to know today that she accepts.

Capitalist: You need an answer today? You know it's Christmas Eve and it's 12:30 pm right now, correct?

Bossman: Yeah, I know. But I just got word from a friend that corporate is thinking about making me take Sparkman from Atlanta as part of a succession plan, and you know what I think about him. So rather than wait on that, we're going to move on Carol, and we need her to accept today, so I can go into the next week and tell them that it's already filled when they call me.

Capitalist: Why don't we just say we have an offer out if that happens and give her a couple of days to think about it?

Bossman: Not good enough. Corporate will make us retract the offer. Get it done today. Gotta go! We're opening some presents! <Click>

After the call, I gathered myself on the reality of demanding a three-hour window to accept an offer on Christmas Eve, and you know what I did? I made the freaking call, boys and girls. It went a little something like this:

Capitalist: Carol! How are you? Kris Dunn from <company name>. Got a couple of minutes to talk? I've got good news...

Carol: Kris, can you repeat that? I'm at church with my kids. They always get so excited around Christmas... (Church bells ringing in the background)

Capitalist: Um, you bet Carol, got great news for you going into the holiday. We want you to join the team, and here's some details for you... (Capitalist outlines broad specs of the deal, selling as hard as he can.)

Carol: Well Kris, that is great news. Send me the offer package, and I'll look it over on Christmas Day and call you back the day after Christmas.

Capitalist: Well Carol, it's funny you say that. Because I'm in a little bit of a pinch here (long, apologetic intro into the issue), and well, I need you to decide by close of business today to accept the offer or not.

Carol: Kris, you know it's Christmas, right? That I'm with my kids? I'm currently in church?

Capitalist: I know. Still, you're the one we want, and we have to close it today to ensure we can bring you aboard.

Carol: <silence for 10 seconds>. Send the package. I'll look at it. Goodbye. (sound of Capitalist trying to apologize again but unable to before hearing <Click>)

And that, boys and girls, is how you know you've arrived in the show. Cost of an Indeed sponsored job? $200-$400 depending on volume. Cost of a third-party recruiter placement? $30K.

The realization you've just crossed a line on Christmas Eve that only Gordon Gekko and Ari Gold could appreciate? Priceless.

P.S.—Carol accepted and rocked the house at our company. I lasted three more years before I couldn't take it anymore. The boss outlasted me before being involuntarily retired by the *Fortune* 500 company, then moved to Hilton Head, where he stays active as a consultant in the same industry and actively nurtures his 318 LinkedIn connections.

4

HR Stereotypes and the Evolution of HR Saying "Yes"

If you're lucky enough to be different, don't ever change.
—Taylor Swift

Why do some people hate HR? It's a great question. Why do some people hate Texas, the Democratic Party, or the New England Patriots? Why are some so vocal about their hatred for Chipotle? Pick a topic in America, and you're likely to get a 50/50 split. It's who we are and what we do. We can't agree on a flavor of gum to buy, but we'll defend your right to buy that gum *all day long*.

What's interesting about HR is that while we have some haters, we don't have a lot of people on the other side walking around saying the following:

> You know, for my money, HR is the leading function in corporate America. Some people like marketing, some people like finance, but I think they're full of s***—HR is where the real talent is.

HR has detractors, but few true fans outside the function. Why is that? If Taco Bell has people of questionable intelligence tattooing its logo on their bodies, why can't we even get a random tweet telling the world we're underrated? Let's dig in.

HR Stereotypes: We've Become a Caricature of a Caricature

The first thing any enterprising HR leader who wants some love has to realize is that the world has already defined our function. There are multiple stereotypes related to our profession that have gained steam in the last sixty years that are alive and well.

Of course, the word "stereotype" doesn't automatically mean the assumptions aren't true. To the contrary, the total sum of our work in the world of HR generally reinforces the world's view of us.

I'm not saying that you're *lame*, but we've done a lot of C+ work. You know what happens in today's world related to C+ work? It gets put on the list of things to be automated, taken over by computers, artificial intelligence, and a robot that engineering named "Nancy" as a shout out to when the company used to have humans in HR.

Nancy is going to be totally cool (I'm a futurist, work with me). The engineers had a great time programming her with HR stereotypes to make sure that everyone felt comfortable when humans in HR were gone. Here's a copy of the message developers at your company will post on GitHub in 2025 related to the specs for Nancy:

August 25, 2025

To: The automation team at GridLoad

From: Charlie

Subject: Specs for Nancy

What up, comrades? OK, great to see our project to automate HR is coming to live status. As we talked about on Slack, we should have a pretty easy time automating HR because what they do is pretty binary. Mostly transactions and a big database of knowledge to pull from. It's ideal for our new AI layer and better yet, the answer to most of the questions is "no."

Here's our roadmap/project plan and what we need to account for to make Nancy seem real to the rest of the team at GridLoad:

1. **There's this big database called the "body of knowledge" from an organization called SHRM.** It includes a bunch of info from topics like compensation, employee relations, and recruiting. I did a word count and it should be completely consumed by our AI layer in just under two days, which will allow Nancy to begin answering questions later this week.

2. **There's also a list of transactions that HR has always done in areas like payroll, etc.** The good news is that the vendors we have traditionally used for those services have advanced to the point where we provide data from the HRIS system and the timecard software solution and payroll just happens.

3. **Other areas of traditional importance involving HR have become similarly automated.** Benefits are a good example—enrollment is now automatic, and to provide the (in)human touch, we're going to do all new hire paperwork with an automated conversation with Nancy in the cloud. Early testing shows that 90 percent of people like it better than a live interaction with HR.

4. **At this point, I know you're thinking: "Charlie, what about all the questions not included in those areas that HR (now Nancy) will have to answer?"** The good news is that I've already uploaded all email conversations that have occurred with HR FTEs from 2008 to 2024 and asked Rick and Ann to spend a day asking Nancy every question they could think of. Nancy started out being able to answer 61 percent of the questions, but she's up to 86 percent as she got smarter about the context behind the questions.

5. **The only thing we need to figure out is the demeanor we want Nancy to have.** Given the fact that HR loved to tell people "no," I wanted her to be a bit dismissive and argumentative, but Rick and Ann thought we should make her nicer. Open to your feedback.

I think we can have Nancy fully functional by early October. Hit me with questions.

—Charlie

Can you be replaced by a robot? Of course not. Do people believe HR is a great place for AI and machine learning to replace humans?

Yes. Yes, they do.

Stereotypes, involving HR being good at policy, transactions, and a very specific body of knowledge, define the average HR pro to most people who rely on our function from the outside. They believe that's the sum of our game. They also believe we're really good at saying no, which makes the future of your job in HR all about saying yes.

If you want to screw Charlie's plan to replace you with Nancy, start saying yes.

Saying "Yes" More as an HR Leader

Let's talk about saying "yes" as an HR pro. The biggest stereotype the world has about HR is that we're the corporate people police, there to say "no" to everything we can.

Our function declines a lot of things inside companies that need a hard "no." The problem, as you'll see when we dig into the 9 Faces of HR, is that a large percentage of our profession is behaviorally wired to say "no"—*to everything.*

Being behaviorally wired to say "no" means you don't say "yes" when you should. The people in our profession who are genetically programmed to say "no" are often the first people your peers in other departments experienced in HR, and as a result, most of the world hasn't experienced a key HR pro or leader looking to say "yes."

How do you say yes more as an HR leader or a line HR Manager? It's simple:

1. Listen to someone's problems. As Jay-Z and ASAP Rocky have explained to us, the business leaders around you have many, many problems.
2. When they ask you for permission to do something that feels icky and risky, resist the urge to say "no."
3. After fighting off the surge of blood to your throat to avoid saying "no," say "yes."
4. After saying "yes," quickly follow the affirmative with a list of things you need them to do to make the "yes" a reality.

Need an example? Let's help a manager looking to fire an employee we'll name "Shirley":

> **Manager:** *"Shirley's killing me. She's gotta go."*
>
> **You (the HR leader/HR pro):** *<huge gulp as you resist the urge to say no>*
>
> **You:** *"I agree, if you say she's gotta go, she's gotta go. You have my support, but here's what I need from you in the next thirty days to get it done."*

Instead of saying "no, you can't, because you haven't done this," you said, "I agree, here's the plan."

You said yes instead of no. You interrupted a ten-year pattern of that manager thinking HR was going to tell them "no." The list of things they need to do to make it happen is exactly the same, but the difference is that you just agreed to partner with them to make it happen.

Saying yes doesn't mean "go crazy, manager." Saying yes means "I support what you want, so here's what I need to help you get that done."

The AI robot that Charlie is building (Nancy) knows how to say no. Charlie can't make it smart enough to deal with everything that has to happen after Nancy says "yes."

This Just In: A Lot of People Are Counting on HR to Say "No"

So you said "yes," rocked their world, and ceased to become a corporate cop. Oddly enough, some of these managers are actually looking for you to say "no."

They've grown addicted to you saying no because it means they don't have to deal with their own s***. You're the excuse, the reason they can't do proactive work on behalf of the mother ship.

Here's a list of things that the managers in your company are counting on you to say "no" to:

» **Firing low performers.** This just in—even though this is one of the biggest complaints related to saying no, many requesting managers are relieved if you say no, primarily because the steps to get there are hard. It's just easier if you say no, especially if they haven't been manager of the year to the person in question.

» **Paying high performers more money.** Behind the scenes, HR is used as an excuse on why we can't do proactive things for great employees. "Want more money? I'd love to give it to you, but any pay increase request out of cycle is going to be denied by HR."

» **Giving the highest rating on a performance review.** One of my favorites is hearing the following from employees: "My manager said she's been told that no one can get the top rating."

» **Not giving someone an annual merit increase.** In order to pay the top performers, you're going to have to take it away from someone else. If you were brave enough to try that as a manager, you forgot one thing—the performance review attached to the zero increase has to match and be brutal. So, we said no.

» **Proactively coaching their employees on tough issues.** We ask to be in those coaching meetings too much. At times that's for good reason, but our need to be part of tough conversations makes the manager move slower, or not at all.

» **Allowing teams to be active on social media.** That's risky, my friend! We can't have people representing the company on social media, right? So our company has a policy, then gets zero impact from one of the most transformative channels of this century.

» **Negotiation of more PTO for a new hire.** Straight up policy police time. Candidate makes the request, hiring manager flips it to us for the "no." As a result they get to say, "it's not me, it's them." Classic.

» **Allowing people to get out of mandatory training because they have real work to do.** A manager has an employee complain they don't have time for training. They flip the exception request to you, get a quick "no," then forward your email to the employee.

The managers you support have grown addicted to HR saying no. When you say "no," it means they're off the hook and don't have to have the hard conversations. They simply report your "no" to the requesting employee or candidate.

They love when you say "no," because the alternative is messy. If you say "yes" and quickly follow it by what you need to execute the yes, the burden is on them.

Start saying "yes" to change the narrative of how you're viewed as an HR leader.

"God's Plan" from Drake Is Telling You How to Do HR

Imagine if I never met the broskis...
—Drake

If you want to break free of HR stereotypes and become mass-market, a good role model is Drake. Hang with me here.

Life with kids these days is hard for a GenX parent. While my wife has temporarily Jedi mind tricked my 14-year-old into loving hits from the 70s and 80s (she drives him around and she may as well have tied him up and made him listen to the Sirius stations that peddle that fare for a year to make that happen), I know the truth:

Rock Is Dead. Hip Hop Is Now the Choice of the Masses.

Some of you will correct me, citing the differences between the pop charts and the actual hip-hop charts. Okay, you got me. I don't follow the scene that closely; I only know from following the habits of my 17-year old son that the 14-year old will defect from his mother's preferences quicker than a Cuban baseball prospect with fifteen minutes of free time in America and a sleeping security guard outside his room at the Courtyard by Marriott.

The reason he defects from his mom's music? Drake. Love him or hate him, Drake understands how to connect in a way that others don't. As soon as our fourteen-year-old is driving whatever old piece of steel I give him, Drake's going to scoop him up like The Beatles did my parents and Nirvana did me.

But I don't hate Drake for the domination. I think HR and recruiting can learn a lot from Drake. Before we talk about that, some stats from Billboard from March of 2018:

» **Drake's "God's Plan"** dominated the Billboard Hot 100 chart for a sixth week (dating to its debut at No. 1), logging a hefty 92.8 million U.S. streams according to Nielsen Music. The song, whose official video arrived Feb. 16, 2018, had now logged two of the top four streaming weeks ever (as of March 2018).

> › 103.1 million U.S. streams, "Harlem Shake," Baauer (driven heavily by viral videos incorporating the song's official audio), chart dated March 2, 2018
> › 101.7 million, "God's Plan," Drake, March 3, 2018
> › 97.6 million, "Harlem Shake," Baauer, March 9, 2018
> › 92.8 million, "God's Plan," Drake, March 10, 2018
> › 84.5 million, "Look What You Made Me Do," Taylor Swift, September 16, 2017
> › 83.3 million, "God's Plan," Drake, . February 10, 2018
> › 82.4 million, "God's Plan," Drake, February 3, 2018
> › 79.6 million, "God's Plan," Drake, February 17, 2018
> › 75.5 million, "God's Plan," Drake, February 24, 2018

That's what we call "results" in the business world. Your HR or recruiting function could learn a lot from Drake. Here's what he does better than other artists and what you could learn from him:

» **Drake understands the streaming industry better than anyone else.** Drake has a Midas touch when it comes to releasing full albums and singles to bridge the attention gap while he's pondering his next full project. Look back at the history, and you'll see a strategy master. The lesson for you? It's not enough in today's frenetic world to revamp your careers site and think you're done. You'll need fresh and frequent campaigns to stand out in the streaming world—even in HR or recruiting.

» **Drake knows how to create a hook.** "God's Plan"? "Hotline Bling"? I could go on. Drake's often mocked by the hard-core hip-hop world, but he understands how to create a mass-market hook better than anyone else in the industry. Your lesson in HR and recruiting? You need to think more like a marketer at all times. Start with this freebie I'll give you: Do a "God's Plan" campaign next week—tell a story about how one of your people did great, selfless work on behalf of a customer or client, then meme the s*** out of that thing on your recruiting channels. Have some fun. Loosen up. Ride the wave. Connect it to great service and random acts of kindness in the workplace. Dare the haters to stand up against the Drake hegemony.

» **Drake's videos are incredibly inclusive.** Drake's videos have a history of showing the common people in them. The "God's Plan" video shows him giving away a million dollars in Miami. You don't have to give away money—you just need to show people coming together, having fun, and being a team that doesn't take themselves too seriously.

» **Drake is a streaming platform agnostic.** He doesn't care which platform gets the results, he's on all of them—Apple, Spotify, etc. You should also be experimenting on all the platforms available—social, video, etc.

» **Drake understands your kids better than you do.** He recently showed up on Twitch to play Fortnite with a famous gamer and almost broke the internet. If it's hot, Drake has no issue co-opting someone else's platform to promote himself. You can take advantage of the same thing by running a Fortnite tournament for the kids of your employees. Most of your employees won't get it, but their kids will think their very uncool folks work at a cool company. Co-opt trends with no shame and you win.

If I see another Instagram post with a Drake meme, I'm going to... Actually, they still make me smile every time I see them.

I can't even hate on Drake's oversaturated Instagram account. Drake understands how to market a brand. HR and recruiting should copy every one of his moves that they can.

5
HR's Big Innovation Problem

Without a deadline, baby, I wouldn't do nothing.
—Duke Ellington

Stereotypes Suck But They're Often True

Stereotypes are awful. Catholics usually go to Notre Dame. People from the South have family trees without branches. White men can't jump.

Of course, behind every stereotype is something that was once widely held to be true. It becomes a stereotype when the subject in question outgrows the conventional practice or wisdom.

Stereotypes can be true and false at the same time. Whether they are unfair or not depends on how far removed we are from the old standard.

Stereotypes are alive and well regarding the HR function. We talked earlier about the preconceived notions held by people who hate HR—notions that they rely on us to perpetrate. Let's run down some more of the basic ones as a warm up here:

» HR is great at the employee handbook.
» HR is the department responsible for the company picnic and party.
» HR has secrets on almost everyone in the company.
» HR is good at something they refer to as the "SHRM Body of Knowledge."

> »   Jan from HR clears out the breakroom daily with the s*** she warms up in the microwave.
> »   If HR schedules a meeting with you, you're getting fired.
> »   You don't go to HR if you want to hear "yes." Better to beg for forgiveness.

Are those things true or not? Probably depends on your company. The bigger issue beyond stereotypes is that HR doesn't lead change in most companies. From my experience, HR is often late to the game when it comes to innovation and driving change.

We should talk about that because it's killing us—and you.

The Arrogance of Being Comfortable with Today

Change happens. We know this across history through countless examples from every industry and every profession. Pick any corner of the business world and you'll see waves of change occurring on a decade by decade basis.

But we're eager to be comfortable with the way we're doing things now; it feels good. Surely it will be good enough for tomorrow as well, right?

It's hard to keep focused on what's next. But if you don't stay focused on emerging trends, you run the risk of extinction.

Need an example? Consider the case of a guy named Bill Gates, who just happens to be one of the most successful founders in the history of Earth. That's right, I just provided context by naming our planet rather than a business sector.

Bill Gates is the founder of Microsoft and through the company's development of its flagship product Windows, dominated the tech industry worldwide in the 1980s and 1990s. Bill Gates has forgotten more about business than people like you and me know, but in 1980 he riffed the quote that appears below about being comfortable with the way things are.

"640K of Memory Should Be Enough for Anybody."

Oops! Gates is talking about the memory in your computer, which in 1981 was measured in kilobytes. In a moment of weakness, he provided this throwaway quote. Of course, required memory soon expanded to megabytes, followed by gigabytes, and now we're tinkering with terabytes.

The Garbage HR Has Said That Sounds Like the 640K of Memory Quote

People in glass houses shouldn't throw stones. It's fun to laugh at the Gates quote until you realize that he's worth ninety-five billion dollars and now spends his days on problems like eliminating the flu from the Earth. Kind of makes your MBO of starting up an HR Twitter account at your company look, well, limited in reach and impact.

Plus, HR people have said some stupid s*** through the years as well. Consider the following gems:

» "I don't see us going away from forms. People need that human touch."

» "Everyone is going to retire by the time they're fifty-five with this stock market run." (said in 2006, before the big recession hit).

» "Family coverage will always be free."

» "This Generation X sure is problematic." (said after they watched the movies Clerks and Singles in the early 90s and obviously before Millennials arrived in the workplace)

» "I know Phil likes to give you a little spank when you walk by. He's just an enthusiastic guy."

» "Don't forget the pension program when you think about that offer. No one can ever take the pension program from you."

» "Why would I need to buy a posting on Monster? My job ads in the paper are great. When I really need to turn it up, I do a display ad."

» "I'm going to hang on to my job board contracts. That Indeed SEO stuff seems a little too hocus pocus for my tastes."

Damn. Look closely at our profession, and you'll find even more gems like these. We can't laugh at anyone! We're completely guilty of holding on to things for too long and generally being wrong about what's going to happen next.

But wait—what if we were open to change and someone could help us understand what's going to happen in one year, three years, or five years? Couldn't we get better with all this future-related stuff?

The Problem with Predicting the Future of HR

In a word? No... The problem with the future is two-fold—1) We're not ready for it or willing to change, and 2) No one has any freaking idea what's going to happen in the future.

To illustrate point number two, let me introduce a data nerd named Philip Tetlock. Tetlock, currently the Annenberg University Professor of Democracy and Citizenship, is a Canadian-American political science writer famous for a piece of meta-analysis called the *Tetlock Study*, summarized in *Expert Political Judgment: How Good Is It? How Can We Know?*.

In the research for that book, Tetlock conducted a set of small-scale forecasting tournaments between 1984 and 2003. The forecasters were 284 experts from a variety of fields, including government officials, professors, journalists, and others, with many opinions, from Marxists to free-marketeers.

The tournaments solicited roughly 28,000 predictions about the future and found the forecasters were often only slightly more accurate than chance, and usually worse than basic extrapolation algorithms, especially on longer-range forecasts three to five years out. Forecasters with the biggest news media profiles were also especially bad.

Tetlock later famously compared the accuracy of the experts to a group of dart-throwing monkeys. That's throwing shade.

Need more proof that no one can accurately forecast the future? Consider the past work of the management consultant firm McKinsey and Company, often cited by *Fortune* 500 companies as the smartest guys/gals in the world. AT&T hired McKinsey in 1980 to forecast cell phone penetration in the U.S. by the year 2000.

They could have called my dad in 1980 (he was a telecom lineman at the time) to kick all the AT&T officers in the groin. He would have done it for half the money.

Here's what happened: McKinsey's prediction for wireless subscribers in 2000 was 900,000 subscribers, which ended up being less than one percent of the actual figure, which was 109 million. Based on this legendary forecast, AT&T decided there was not much of a future in wireless.

A decade later, AT&T had to acquire McCaw Cellular for $12.6 billion to get back in the game. There are almost nine billion wireless connections worldwide as I write this book.

Oopsie!

If Someone Tells You What Is Innovative in HR, That Kind of Defeats the Purpose, Right?

So, we've set the stage and told you that we're bad at predicting the future and generally comfortable with the status quo in HR, just like our peers in other functional areas. We also know that change is happening at a wild pace, and a future boss is going to expect HR pros to be innovative and come up with solutions to big problems on the fly.

This just in—no one is going to tell us what being innovative looks like. There's no road map because every situation is different. What's innovative in my company may be pedestrian in yours. You might over-engineer a solution to a business problem at your organization and look like an academic fool rather than a pragmatic partner.

Being innovative is like art and style—you know it when you see it.

A big trend in performance management over the last decade is to reduce rating scales from five points to three points. The logic in this trend is to increase the quality of conversations between manager and employee and simply focus on the difference between "good" and "great."

But even when you reduce points on a rating scale, you're still left with this funky question asked by countless employees:

"How do I get a 3"? (or a "5" or whatever the highest rating is on any performance review item)

For many companies intent on forcing a merit matrix distribution or performance curve on their employee population, the answer has been, *"no one here gets a 5,"* which is about as debilitating of an answer as you can hear as an employee.

The real answer must be a set of behaviors that are in place for someone to innovative. Display curiosity, try new solutions, attempt to improve the status quo in the area in question—not once, but as a normal part of your day as if it's embedded in your DNA.

Translation: If I have to tell you how to be innovative, you're not innovative.

Doing more transactions and running processes more efficiently isn't going to make that future boss think you're awesome in HR. In fact, it will probably mean the exact opposite to them.

Bonus

Jedi Mind Tricks from Salesforce.com "Equality Matters as Much as Diversity"

While we're on the topic of innovation, let's talk about the marketplace of ideas (buzzword alert). Let's face it—HR could be a lot better at marketing.

Some primary areas come to mind when you start brainstorming all the marketing opportunities HR has. Recruiting marketing, culture branding, recognition, and corporate social responsibility (CSR) all come to mind.

If you're going to be perceived as innovative, you're going to need to market what you do well more effectively.

But marketing only goes so far when your product sucks. When the product is bad, marketing might not be enough—you might need public relations (PR) work.

PR is about spin, about getting your story out there to frame the way you're perceived. Normal PR takes talking points and seeks to distribute the story. But transformative PR (and maybe HR) goes much further than that.

Example—If you don't like the answer, you can always change the question. Especially if you have money. Lots of money.

Framing Means You Control the Narrative

Case in point—there are a lot of companies across America that struggle with diversity hiring. Those companies are generally under-utilized in multiple-job families, and even as they try to attract diverse talent, it hasn't gone well. After all, there aren't enough candidates (pipeline issues), and not everyone wants to work for your company. Throw in the fact that you can't pay new hires anything they want without messing up your compensation equity, and most companies don't make the progress they'd like to.

Tech companies in Silicon Valley have a huge diversity hiring issue for all the aforementioned reasons.

Salesforce (the mighty CRM giant) is one of those companies. But Salesforce is smarter than you and me and doesn't limit their thinking to today's conventional wisdom on human capital issues.

Salesforce looked at the diversity hiring issue and did what any company with loads of cash would do. They changed the answer and thus the question.

Turns out the answer (as reimagined by Salesforce) isn't more diversity, it's more equality.

Confused? You'll get it soon.

The Great Salesforce Drive for Pay Equity

To give credit where credit is due, Salesforce CEO Marc Benioff revealed that his company spent about three million dollars in 2015 to equalize compensation across the company, closing the tech giant's gender pay gap. Here's a rundown of that move from *The Atlantic*:

> In a panel at a conference organized by *Fortune* last week, Marc Benioff, the CEO of the cloud-based software company Salesforce, said that he recently ordered a review of

all 17,000 employees' salaries to see if female employees' pay was in line with those of male employees doing similar jobs. According to *Fortune*, Benioff said that the company is spending about $3 million extra this year on its payroll to make these adjustments. "We can say we pay women the same that we pay men," he said at the conference. "We looked at every single salary."

Salesforce didn't provide deeper details, but that's why you have me. So, let's break it down.

First, the easy math—if all 17,000 employees (2015 headcount at the time) got an adjustment and three million dollars was spread out among them, that would be an average adjustment of 176 dollars.

Of course, that's not the right math. Assume half of those employees are female, and only females got the adjustment, and that brings the average adjustment to 353 dollars.

But wait! The article from *The Atlantic* (and other sources) lets us know that Salesforce at the time was only thirty percent female, so that means 5,100 female employees splitting the three million dollars for an average of 588 dollars.

What does all that mean? Well, if the analysis was full, complete and accurate—and we have no reason to believe it wasn't, based on the reputation of Salesforce—it means they didn't have much of an issue with gender pay equity. Also, we know that things like this are never spread evenly; there were undoubtedly pockets in Salesforce that didn't look great, and female employees within these pockets got the majority of the adjustments, much higher than the average cited in the last math example that I provided.

The Salesforce Pivot: It's About Equality, Not Diversity

This statement from Benioff says it all: "*We can say we pay women the same that we pay men, we looked at every single salary.*" Once you can make that statement, you can start playing offense and stop playing defense.

Salesforce was playing offense with the outside world soon thereafter, starting with the hiring of a chief equality officer. More on this hiring and the positioning of the hiring from a *TechCrunch* article in 2016:

> It's important for tech companies to have at least one voice at the senior leadership table that advocates for issues around equality, diversity, and inclusion. Unfortunately, that's just not the case for many companies in the tech industry. Salesforce, a company that said a year ago that a major focus for it was "the women's issue," recently became an exception to the rule with the hiring of Tony Prophet, its first-ever chief equality officer. Two weeks into his role, Prophet sat down to chat about Salesforce's evolution from a focus on diversity and inclusion to an overall focus on equality.
>
> "The notion of being chief equality officer—now that was very thoughtful and deliberate on Salesforce's part and on Marc's [Benioff] part versus being chief of diversity or chief of inclusion because you can have a diverse workplace or a diverse culture in many parts of America that are very diverse but are hardly inclusive and there's hardly equality," Prophet told me. "We want to go beyond diversity and beyond inclusion to really achieve equality."

Translation? Game, set, match.

Salesforce Is Playing Chess; The Rest of Us Are Playing Checkers

Let's dig into the logic. If you can't make strides on diversity but can afford to achieve equality when it comes to pay, odds are people are going to be a lot less critical of you for your diversity shortcomings.

Translation: The company still has a lot of work to do, but by changing the conversation to equality, not diversity, they've effectively changed how they're measured by the outside world.

I'm not saying diversity hiring in tech isn't important. I am saying that Salesforce is working towards a related, equally important goal and now will be considered in a different light than other major tech companies, whom I expect will follow suit soon enough.

If you can't find enough diverse hires, it makes sense to ensure all (including women) are paid on equal footing to everyone else.

Then you obviously want to get your message out.

At Salesforce, that message includes the fact they're changing the conversation from diversity to equality, with an emphasis on pay equity. Salesforce created a master stroke to relieve some of the diversity hiring pressure and is going all in with first mover advantage and everything that comes with it.

I'm a cynic on most things. But even the cynic in me has to respect how Salesforce is controlling the narrative in this area.

Sometimes innovation in HR is a straight line. Sometimes it's as simple as reframing the question and doing great stuff in a big area of need while you work on a harder problem.

Don't forget to tell the world about the good stuff.

6

How the 9 Face of HR Model Works

You're more beautiful than Cinderella. You smell like
pine needles, and you have a face like sunshine.
—Becca (Ellie Kemper) in *Bridesmaids* (2011)

The 9 Faces of HR is a model that I first brainstormed as a natural extension of the consulting world's 9-box grid and the HR world's performance vs. potential model (see the next chapter for a deeper dive on both models).

The smartest people I know steal ideas from others and tweak them to fit their needs. I started with these models in mind and then mixed other ideas and experiences in, like an old-school rapper sampling clips of Sinatra, Madonna, and Barry White in the same song.

I miss the wide-open sampling days from the music industry. Of course, I miss Napster and LimeWire as well. I guess it makes sense for people to get paid for their original work, although some would say there are no new ideas.

The 9 Faces of HR is a labor of love developed over a decade. Whether you love it or think it's absolute bulls***, I'm convinced I've completely nailed this model and guide to the personalities that make up and drive performance in the world of HR.

Enjoy, my HR nerd friends.

The 9 Faces of HR Model (and What It Means)

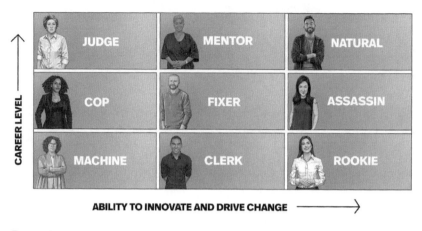

Figure 6.1. The 9 Faces of HR Model

The 9 Faces of HR model takes every active HR professional and divides them up across nine distinct personas.

Millions of HR professionals, but only 9 Faces. Look at the 9 Faces of HR graphic we just showed you, and you'll see a 9-box grid. We determine which face you are by evaluating two things—career level in HR and ability to innovate, drive change, and add value—which are represented across the X and Y axis of this grid:

1. **Your HR Career Level.** The first factor providing a coordinate to your position in the 9 Faces of HR is your career level. Are you early career (bottom row), mid-career (middle row), or senior level (top row) as an HR professional?

   The savvy HR pro understands that there are many shades of gray in this determination. As someone who recruits extensively for a living, I can tell you it becomes easier the more HR resumes and HR LinkedIn profiles you see and evaluate. The right designation in this area becomes a combination of title, experience level, and company size.

   Titles are tricky, which is why experience and company size must be considered when determining career level in the 9 Faces of HR model. HR assistant, coordinator, and representative roles generally fall to the early career designation. HR manager titles become trickier as they generally fall mid-career level, but single person HR shops are often manned by early career HR pros with this title who have less experience than that title would suggest.

HR director and the VP of HR are just as tricky. VP of HR titles scream "senior level," but title inflation in small companies means that not all VPs of HR have the same experience and knowledge. Some would say HR director means a mid-level HR pro, but this title exists and is occupied by some incredible HR pros with twenty or more years of experience at big jobs in big companies.

That's why title alone can't drive your career level position in the 9 Faces of HR. To properly slot you, we need your title, your experience level, the size of your company, the number of people you manage, and the car you drive.

Just kidding about the car. Unless you drive a Saab, which indicates you're obviously senior level and incredibly pretentious.

2. **Your Ability to Innovate, Drive Change, and Add Incremental Value.** Once we've established your career level, we complete your placement within the 9 Faces of HR model by evaluating your ability to innovate, drive change, and add incremental value within the organization you serve (low, mid, and high in this area moves left to right across the columns in the grid).

We do this with a mix of assessment factors that will be discussed at length in later chapters of this book. Find the complete rundown of that methodology in those chapters, and refer to the DNA maps for each one of the 9 Faces of HR to see the mix of cognitive and behavioral factors that makes each persona in this model unique.

How I Came Up with the 9 Faces of HR Model

I'm an HR nerd just like you. I also happen to be one of two owners at Kinetix, an RPO recruiting firm headquartered in Atlanta (doing work nationally on behalf of some great clients).

My experience as an HR pro is clear. I climbed the corporate HR ladder quicker than most because I had an eye for what was "next," and I liked to package HR products and projects in a way that could be marketed effectively. People have used the following to describe me, and I have always taken it as a compliment:

"You're not like other HR people I've known."

Flash forward to me investing in and joining Kinetix in 2010. Our recruiting model at Kinetix is based on specialty recruiters. We recruit across all industries and functional areas, including HR. As an HR pro, I took special interest in the trends that were evident in the HR searches (at the managerial, directorial, and VP level) at Kinetix. I used the reach of my blogs (*The HR Capitalist, Fistful of Talent*) to land additional searches that contributed to this model.

One trend became apparent in the world of HR search:

Nobody pays a search firm to find a stereotypical and traditional HR pro.

As I dug into the HR searches we had over time, the trend was easy to see. Intake calls for the searches were clear—people were paying for an HR search because they were not satisfied with the status quo and were looking for a different type of HR pro. They were looking for someone with the ability to innovate, drive change, and add value they didn't expect or ask for. They just didn't know how to find this type of candidate.

With that reality in mind, we started using an assessment tool that included a cognitive dimension and seven behavioral dimensions. I liked the tool because eight total dimensions provided depth without unnecessary complexity. We started using this validated assessment in every HR search we did.

As we interviewed the candidates, heard their experiences and stories, and evaluated them for open HR jobs, we cross-referenced what we were hearing with the assessment. We submitted final candidates to clients and got their feedback related to the match with what they were looking for.

The trend was clear. Candidates with demonstrated or perceived ability to innovate, drive change, and add incremental value (our view as well as our clients) had specific behavioral profiles.

As a result of this process, the 9 Faces of HR model is based on over fifty searches for which I've used the aforementioned methodology.

Notes on Validation of this Model

Of course, you ask about validation of the model. I expect nothing less from my HR colleagues.

The complete assessment platform we used has heavy validation. Our use of that validated assessment model to dig into the HR manager, director, and VP candidates' ability to innovate, drive change, and add value has not been validated.

If that's enough to make you wag your finger at me, you should stop reading now. Seriously.

I've spent a lot of time with candidates in the world of HR. I've done the work. I've heard what people are looking for. The behavioral markers you'll see when you get to the individual chapters detailing each persona in the 9 Faces of HR are real.

I don't need validation study to tell me there's ROI in using the phone over email in recruiting, or that the more questions I ask my kids about a single topic or situation, the closer I get to the complete truth. I just know.

I've nailed it with this model. If you need validation, see the receptionist and she'll make sure your parking ticket gets the stamp.

Related: If you wag your finger at me due to validation, I also know which one of the 9 Faces of HR you are.

Bottom Left Doesn't Mean You Lose

A cautionary note before you read the rest of this book. There's no such thing as good or bad related to the 9 Faces of HR. The most important thing is that you work to get a feel for which one of the faces you are, then find a company, job, or manager who gets you and seeks to maximize what you are great at.

Whether you're identified as a "The Cop" or "The Natural," you can, and will, contribute to great HR outcomes.

But a day is coming for all of us when we get a new boss, and that boss isn't sure whether we're good at this whole HR thing. At that point, having the self-awareness that comes with knowing which face you are is a huge advantage because you can understand how you transmit clues about what's most important to you as an HR pro and seek to maximize or minimize those signals based on who you are talking to.

I love HR. You do great work. Let's keep exploring the 9 Faces of HR.

7

The Great BS Artists Who Gave Us the 9-Box Grid and Performance vs. Potential

The only thing that we need to figure out is what makes them think they can't live without us for the next three years.
—Marty Kann (Don Cheadle) in *House of Lies*

As much as I thought about skipping this chapter to make this book a little lighter, I can't. My experience sharing the 9 Faces of HR at conferences and events tells me that less than 50 percent of the people who will read this book are well-versed in the 9-box grid, a staple of high-end management consultants everywhere that has been hijacked by the human capital industry.

If you're not sure what the 9-box grid is, don't sweat it. It doesn't make you inferior to your peers in any way. In fact, by the end of this chapter, I'll have parodied the model in ninety-nine ways, which is kind of a sign that while the model has great utility, it should be openly and routinely mocked.

If you are well versed in all things 9-box grid-related, feel free to skim this. If not, you should read it because it might save your ass with a new boss at some point in the next 5–10 years.

McKinsey: They Messed Up the AT&T Wireless Prediction, But Gave Us the 9-Box Grid

Remember management consultant firm McKinsey and Company from the last chapter? Though often cited as the smartest guys/girls in the room, we used their work for AT&T related to predicting wireless subscriber growth as proof that predicting the future was an impossible task.

If you work at a *Fortune* 500 company, McKinsey has likely helped your C-level and board of directors on a wide range of strategy issues. You didn't see this work as a worker bee until your company announced an acquisition, shuttered an entire division, or announced a new focus on something cryptic, like "the Internet."

The birth of the 9-box grid went something like this: as the economy became more and more global in the late twentieth century, companies began to struggle with managing large numbers of diverse business units profitably. In response, management thinkers like McKinsey generated models to help simplify decisions that had to be made. One that arose in the early 1970s was the GE–McKinsey 9-box grid.

Your executives might be smart. They might be dumb. But they all like pictures.

The 9-box grid used by McKinsey offered a systematic approach for the decentralized corporation to determine where best to invest its cash. Using this system, a company can judge a unit by two factors that will determine whether it's going to do well in the future: the attractiveness of the industry and the unit's competitive strength within that industry.

> Can you just draw me a picture of what the hell you are talking about?

Companies use the 9-box grid to line up their divisions and business units by plotting on a grid similar to the one below:

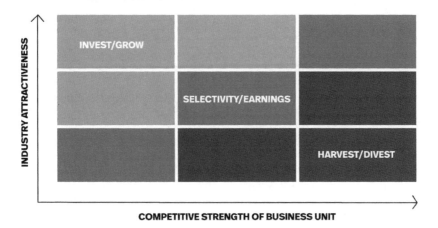

Figure 7.1. McKinsey's 9-Box Grid

Note: The goal is to be in the top right box of any 9-box grid. Being "top-right" in the McKinsey 9-Box means your division or unit receives funding, investment, and attention. Being "bottom-left" means you're checking your severance agreement as a division president because you're likely to be sold, liquidated, or if you're lucky, run purely for cash. Judgment is obviously required to weigh the trade-offs of positions involved that are not "top-right" or "bottom-left.

Welcome to the show, kids! Grow or die!

Before you take any of this too seriously, remember that McKinsey would have rated the attractiveness of the wireless industry as "low" based on their infamous 1980s projection of future wireless growth.

Or, as the McKinsey partners running that engagement said, "my bad."

The Holy Grail of Performance Management—
Performance vs. Potential

If there's an area in which the average HR department has struggled, it's performance management. It's not because you're inferior as an

HR leader or HR pro. It's because doing performance management well requires you to herd temperamental cats while educating those same cats to display perfect judgment on when to scratch and when to purr.

A list of challenges facing the average HR leader trying to get through a performance management cycle:

» Do your people know what they are being measured on?

» Are your managers smart enough to know how employee A is different from employee B?

» Do your managers understand the process and your system for rating employees? Can they accurately contrast the performance of different employees?

» Can your managers be organized enough to complete reviews while they do their day job? Can they write statements to support the ratings given that give creditability to the process?

» Do your managers struggle with positive rating bias towards people who are extremely hot? (You're still reading! That was a test. Kind of.)

» Can your managers sit down with an employee to deliver the review and own their feedback in a one-on-one session?

» Does your executive team even care about this process at your company?

Hard times. Most of you reading this book have lived through this. It's incredibly hard to get the reviews complete, to say nothing of the overall quality of those reviews.

Somewhere along the way, a smart HR leader (or consultant) decided to rise above the mosh pit of activity related to performance appraisals and asked the following question:

> Hey, what would happen if I used the McKinsey 9-Box and just changed the X and Y axis to show which employees (rather than business units) we should invest in?

Translation: We've got to draw them a picture to get them excited! Maybe add some unicorns and rainbows!

And just like that, the *performance vs. potential 9-box grid* was born.

It's unclear who first invented or used the performance vs. potential 9-box grid. Figure 7.2 shows the HR-centric 9-box, with notes on what you need to know below it.

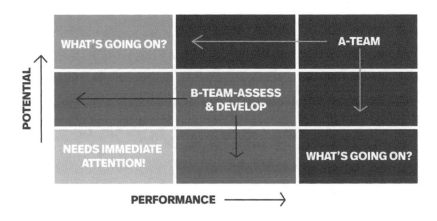

Figure 7.2. The Performance vs Potential Grid

What you need to know about the performance vs. potential grid:

» **We've traded out "attractiveness of industry" and "competitive strength in industry"** in the original McKinsey 9-Box for "performance" and "potential."

» **When plotting employees on this grid, performance is widely considered to be an employee's performance in their job, and potential can mean different things to different companies,** including proprietary succession factor ratings, potential factor ratings, or even ratings related to company values.

» **The dots on the chart above are meant to mesmerize executives!** Each dot represents an employee, and pictures are powerful. The first question you'll hear related to a picture like this is, "tell me who's the dot in the top right," and its companion, "Who's the dot in the bottom left?"

» **While cool, the whole performance vs. potential thing is still very much a garbage in, garbage out exercise,** meaning you have to be good at performance management for it to have true meaning.

» **The grid itself is useful for getting improvements across managers related to the performance process.** If a manager is known for giving more high ratings than reality suggests on his team, telling him that you're going to show the whole department on the 9-box but color code the dots by manager has a way of awakening that manager to the need to be a bit tougher on performance.

If you haven't explored using the performance vs. potential 9-box grid, you should. It's one of the simplest ways an HR leader can move from being viewed as transactional to being viewed as strategic.

I know, I know. Just because you plot dots on a 9-box grid doesn't mean you're strategic.

But if your big tracking metric today is "percentage of reviews completed," maybe you could use the makeover the 9-box provides, right?

Real Talk: What the Boxes Really Mean in the Performance vs. Potential 9-Box

For all its sleekness, the performance vs. potential (I'll call it PvP from here on out) 9-box grid isn't that deep. While pictures are effective for moving people to dialogue and action, they're also tools that reinforce stereotypes and quick-draw judgments on the fly.

Here's what each box in the PvP 9-box grid really means to people evaluating talent through the tool (organized by nickname):

1. **Topper!** (high performer, low potential)—You've topped out. We love what you're doing in the role, but there are some limitations to further advancement based on how you are wired. We're going to call you a Subject Matter Expert (SME), which is true, but you should prepare to spend the next decade in your current job, which might be automated (FYI) in three years. Yes, we see someone moved your Red Stapler. (Time reserved in every hour of succession/performance meetings talking about Toppers: less than one minute.)

2. **Ditch Digger!** (mid performer, low potential)—Just like Topper, we can't see you going much further. That's the good news. The bad news is that you'll receive less praise and rewards than Topper because you're doing less with what God gave you, which, let's face it, is clearly measured by our version of potential. (Time reserved in every hour of succession/performance meetings talking about Ditch Diggers: less than one minute.)

3. **Zombie!** (low performer, low potential)—*"What is this person still doing here?" "Who manages her?"* If you had a dollar for every time someone asked you these questions when you fired up the 9-box on PowerPoint, you'd be driving a Tesla instead of a Toyota. (Time reserved in every hour of succession/performance meetings talking about Zombies: ten minutes or all of it.)

4. **Citizen!** (high performer, mid potential)—No one draws more positive head nodding in meetings than the Citizen. The Citizen makes the most of their talent and might have a little bit more to give, which means they can be trusted in the organization. They're highly likely to win the company values award and the trip to Orange County that goes with it. Then your execs will decide to force promote them to run collections for the rest of their lives. Good times. (Time reserved in every hour of succession/performance meetings talking about Citizens: five minutes.)

5. **Glue!** (mid performer, mid potential)—What's up Glue? Being in the middle box of the 9-box grid isn't good, it isn't bad, it just is. You're doing average work, and you've got average potential. We need you, by the way, so don't leave. We're going to sprinkle some recognition in there once in a while and won't get too worked up when you act out a bit. Did we mention there are annual merit increases? We good? Awesome. (Time reserved in every hour of succession/performance meetings talking about Glue People: less than one minute.)

6. **Stoner!** (low performer, mid potential)—Stoners are maddening for their penchant for showing occasional flashes of brilliance in their job, only to return to sending emails with typos and showing no organizational savvy in their daily interactions. How long we let you stay depends on how often you show the flashes, mixed with how bad your screw-ups hurt us. (Time reserved in every hour of succession/performance meetings talking about Stoners: five minutes.)

7. **Superstar!** (high performer, high potential)—Holding the top right real estate in the PvP 9-box grid means you're the chosen one. You could literally throw up on your manager's desk after a hard night on the town and we'd blame your manager. Our potential-measuring tools say you've got what it takes to promote more than 2X above your current role or to go run the Clarksville, TN, location. Hope your spouse is ready to relocate because you're probably going to have to go to the desert (Clarksville) before you can come back to the corporate mother ship. (Time reserved in every hour of succession/performance meetings talking about Naturals: thirty minutes or all of it.)

8. **Slacker!** (mid performer, high potential)—We did too much for you, didn't we? The Slacker is the kid you know has talent but grew up with everything and now wants to do nothing. The company is your parent. We think you can rule the

world—and you can—but all you want to do it smoke weed and chill. Since we love you (and you have high potential), you can stay around forever, but we'll go through cycles in which we're frustrated with each other. (Time reserved in every hour of succession/performance meetings talking about Slackers: ten minutes.)

9. **Hostage!** (low performer, high potential)—Who is this talented individual's manager? That's the first question you'll hear with the low performing and high potential "hostage" because there's so much potential here it can't possibly be the employee's fault. Companies going hardcore on succession programs will call the manager with the audacity to rate this person lowly on the carpet, resulting in top performance ratings in the next cycle (regardless of performance change). Could it be that the drive/initiative of the "hostage" is faulty? We'll never know because the manager in question "fixed" the glitch. (Time reserved in every hour of succession/performance meetings talking about Hostages: ten minutes.)

The management consulting greats gave us the 9-box grid. The smartest HR pros ripped that model off and created "performance vs. potential," changing how performance and succession are considered in countless companies.

It's only fitting that I ripped off both models to create the 9 Faces of HR. Let's keep digging in.

8

HR Nerd Alert: The Four Factors That Drive the Ability to Innovate, Add Value, and Drive Change in HR

My mama told me when I was young
We are all born superstars
She rolled my hair and put my lipstick on
In the glass of her boudoir
—Lady Gaga in *Born This Way*

In developing the 9 Faces of HR model, we thought about multiple ways to measure ability to *innovate, drive change, and add value*. We determined our best path was to observe what we were seeing in HR candidates for open searches we were conducting (described in Chapter 6) across a variety of behavioral factors.

We used behavioral factors because behavioral assessments are a tool that most HR pros have used, are comfortable with, and have access to. It should be noted that while there are hundreds of behavioral assessments in the market to select from, the validity of most of those tools is based on the same body of research called the "five-factor model."

The trend of the work we did was clear. Four factors emerged to measure directionally an HR Pro's *ability and willingness to innovate, drive change, and add incremental value,* including the following:

1. Cognitive Ability/Processing Speed
2. Assertiveness
3. Rules Orientation
4. Detail Orientation

While the behavioral dimensions listed above are called many different things by assessment companies (more of a preference or marketing decision), assertiveness, rules orientation, and detail orientation are generally included in some capacity in any behavioral assessment you purchase. Cognitive ability is not behavioral in nature and, as a result, may or may not be included in your assessment package.

We used this approach to measure ability/willingness to innovate, drive change, and add value so that readers of this book can self-evaluate with the assessment platform they use if desired.

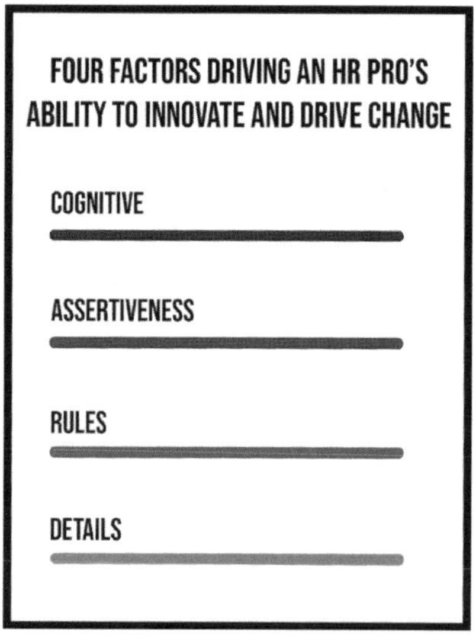

FOUR FACTORS DRIVING AN HR PRO'S
ABILITY TO INNOVATE AND DRIVE CHANGE

COGNITIVE

ASSERTIVENESS

RULES

DETAILS

Figure 8.1. First Look Scorecard

I know. You really want to dig into this part of the 9 Faces of HR model because you're a complete HR nerd.

The following chapters will provide a complete rundown of these dimensions and why they are important to the 9 Faces of HR model. In addition, upcoming chapters detailing each of the nine personas within the 9 Faces of HR model will include charts of how that face breaks down across these four factors.

9
Professional Tourette's Is Dangerous (Cognitive Skills)

The speed of the boss is the speed of the team.
—Lee Iacocca

Everybody thinks they're smart. That's true in all walks of life, including HR.

What if it wasn't about being smart? What if it was simply about speed in the modern workplace?

This chapter is tough to write because no one wants to tell anyone they're slow.

I know YOU'RE fast. Let's talk about the other folks.

Let's Define Cognitive Skills and Processing Speed

The definition of cognitive skills and processing speed I'm using for the 9 Faces of HR model is simple. Cognitive skills in this model means how quickly a candidate or employee will learn, the complexity of work you can give them, how quickly an individual can solve problems, and a host of other items.

Being high on cognitive skills and processing speed is a good thing. It means you're a very quick learner. Mental speed will not be an issue, and new processes or concepts will be grasped quickly. At times, your speed may frustrate others (especially those who score lower is this area) by communicating too quickly or by making quick decisions that appear to be made with little consideration or planning.

I know—you're thinking, *"yeah, I know what to do so fast it probably does frustrate other people."*

Being low on cognitive skills and processing speed isn't a death sentence. It simply means you may really struggle in situations where processing data on the fly or making quick decisions (with the expectation of high accuracy) is required.

Pick the Shape that Best Represents a Continuation of the Pattern Below

What the … If you've seen the directions listed above recently, odds are that you are one of the following:

»   An **industrial psychologist** geeking out in the lab while creating some new assessment designed to protect the world from bad hires. Godspeed to you, Skippy.

»   A **candidate who just wanted to apply for a job**, but you're being asked to do mental gymnastics before you can get to the interview stage. Grrrr …

»   An **HR pro taking an assessment to decide if it's right for your organization**, and now you're worried about your own score. Rightfully so, by the way.

»   An **applicant being assessed for inclusion in a government program called Treadstone**. You aren't sure about the program, but **that guy you met in the lobby named David Webb sure seemed nice**, right? (Young people check out the Jason Bourne trilogy to understand the reference.)

Since you're not a lethal killing machine, you don't have a PhD (most of you, stop reading now if you do), and you're reading this book—you're probably an HR pro. And if you recently read the instructions detailed in the title of this section or something like it, it means the assessment you were taking had a *cognitive component.*

Mama Always Said Life Was Like a Box of Chocolates

If you score low on the cognitive component to any assessment you take related to your employment, *does that mean you're stupid?*

That's a loaded question. As someone who uses an assessment with a cognitive component on a weekly—if not daily—basis, I'm quick to answer no. I don't care what the PhD types will tell me about that because linking a cognitive score in the workplace with the concept of smart vs. stupid or IQ is a quick way to lose talent and friends.

I prefer to think about the cognitive dimension as measuring the ability to learn. Some of you will no doubt challenge that assessment. To you, I say "Google," which means that Google *the company* has agreed with my assessment in the past. Here's a reference to the cognitive dimension in employment screening from an interview with former Google CHRO Laszlo Bock from 2014. This interview with Bock indicated *ability to learn on the fly* was the number one hiring criteria at Google:

> There are five hiring attributes we have across the company... If it's a technical role, we assess your coding ability, and half the roles in the company are technical roles. For every job, though, the No. 1 thing we look for is general cognitive ability, and it's not I.Q. It's learning ability. It's the ability to process on the fly. It's the ability to pull together disparate bits of information.

That represents my safe place for explaining the cognitive dimension to candidates and employees alike. People with high cognitive scores have the ability to take in large amounts of data and make quick, accurate decisions. Many cognitive portions of an assessment feature a timer on the screen and a progress monitor indicating you probably won't finish all the items in the timed portion of the assessment. #SucksToBeYou

The timer is there to put pressure on you to be quick. People with high cognitive scores have the ability to get through a higher number of these questions while answering correctly. People with low cognitive scores do poorly on this type of section because they need time to process and contemplate before making a decision on the items in front of them. The timer doesn't help.

How to Spot a Low Cognitive Teammate (Without Really Trying)

I took a major cognitive assessment eight years ago and scored very high. I'M NEVER TAKING A COGNITIVE ASSESSMENT AGAIN UNLESS MY FAMILY IS HUNGRY AND I HAVE TO. Once you get that high score, you never want to take one again—just in case your score is not—um—repeatable.

But you don't need an assessment to spot a teammate on the "low cog" spectrum. Totally unscientific, but my observations about teammates who score in the bottom half of the bell curve for cognitive processing speed are pretty consistent.

Those candidates usually display the following:

- **They have a two to three second delay when a lot of data is flying in while they're a part of the conversation.** There's a rapid-fire conversation going on, and someone hits them with data and then the conversation stops. The obvious expectation is that they contribute to the dialogue. There's a delay. Their preference is to take their time on the analysis. The pregnant pause is noticeable by those around them, and over time, by the individual in question.

» **They may develop a form of Professional Tourette's,** which I define as someone who's trying to speed up their processing time by quickly blurting out conversational reactions that really don't match the conversation going on (against their natural preference to take their time and come back later with analysis). I see this happening a lot once low cog teammates understand that speed is preferred by the team they're on. They've attempted to do things on the fly, and their response is just a bit off—the contextual understanding isn't there. They needed more time.

It doesn't mean the low cog person isn't smart and can't contribute. It simply means that they'd like to contemplate and think through their answers a bit.

Unfortunately, everything is moving faster in the twenty-first century. When's the last time you had someone tell you they were looking to hire someone who "really took their time and didn't rush?"

Rarely. That's why low cog people are trying to run faster, often with poor results.

How to Spot a High Cognitive Teammate (Without Really Trying)

How do you spot a high cog teammate? It's simple: just look for what I like to call "that guy" (or gal):

1. Finishes other people's sentences
2. Interrupts others
3. Brags about multi-tasking skills
4. Does a Rubik's Cube while listening to classical music AND fully participating on a conference call
5. Frustrates others by their need to make decisions before all the data is present

That last one is key. High cog people have a reputation for making decisions too quickly in some organizations. The career coach for this eager beaver would give him technical advice to "slow the hell down" and "stop making so many damn enemies."

Show-offs, those high cogs. Also, decidedly unaware of how they're being perceived.

Your HR Team Wears a Lot of Different Hats, Right?

Being low cog isn't a death sentence—although it might be at Google based on the earlier quote. Low cog teammates can contribute great things—they just need managers who put them in a position to succeed and don't expect them to win speed contests.

They'll win the mental version of the 10K or the marathon. Just be sure to enter them in a race they can win.

There's room for all cognitive and processing speeds in the 9 Faces of HR and the modern HR team.

Bonus

Revenue per Employee and the Emerging Title of "HR Capologist"

Since we're on the topic of cognitive skills and processing speed, let's talk about HR metrics and analytics.

Any meaningful conversation about HR metrics should be tied to budget season— yes, that soul-sucking process where your operators try to hide Full-time Employees (FTEs) and your finance department slowly cuts them down to size. Because let's face it: the operators you support are addicted to not filling open headcount as a means to make budget.

You've seen this movie before. But the sequels seem to feature a much meaner finance department, which means your operators have no hope of keeping the FTE fat in their budget.

The New Hot Job Is HR Capologist

This means you have a golden opportunity to emerge with a new title: *HR capologist*.

What's a HR capologist, you ask? Let me explain.

Professional sports are filled with quantitative analysts ("quants" for short) who are replacing old school scouts as the pivotal talent manager in any sports franchise—and the new wave of number-driven talent evaluators are called *capologists*. Most professional sports leagues have salary caps, and the goal of the capologist is to ensure

75

that the franchise is making smart decisions about whom they bring aboard and what they pay them.

Brad Pitt movies have been made about this (see *Moneyball*). The stats in baseball and basketball that help identify hidden value are called things like Wins Above Replacement (WAR), and they matter—a lot.

Hate sports? Stay with me for a second because it has more to do with HR than you think.

What goes on with salary caps in sports is important to the HR/talent leader for the following reasons:

» **Your salary cap in HR is your company's salary budget after finance whacks it down to size.** You've got a cap people—time to start embracing your inner geek.

» **The pressure is on to do more with less. It's been that way for a while, right?** Maybe you ought to start helping your operators do something other than complain about it. You talk about Organization Development (OD) stuff; this is your chance to do real OD.

» **Your most effective lever against your company's "salary cap" is revenue per employee (RPE).** If you get more revenue per employee, your company wins. As I've pitched before, the great thing about RPE is that whatever you think you excel in as an HR talent leader (hiring, training, performance management, etc.), you can use your specialty to get more revenue out of the same total spend on people.

» **In sports, more wins for the same or less money is the result of good capology.** In corporate America, production as measured by more revenue per employee is the equivalent of wins.

The HR capologist does one of two things:

1. **They do more with the same or less while hiring like they always have**—this is what I outlined above. Use what you

are good at in HR to get more revenue per employee—it's real world OD.

2. **They start looking for cheaper talent that can do a lot (proportionally) to what traditional talent can do.** Can you find talent that can perform 85 percent of what the incumbent can do for 65 percent of the cost? If so, then you're a natural HR capologist.

Want to start looking into being an HR capologist in your current role? Start publishing RPE numbers and then start having lots of conversations with your operators about how to improve that metric to get more out of the salary cap they've been given.

Time to geek it up and let the conversations drive where you go next. Those conversations are natural places for the high cognitive HR pro to thrive. There are no rules, and the observations are going to come at two hundred miles per hour.

If you're a high cognitive HR pro, you have a chance to be a HR capologist.

But You Think Revenue Per Employee Doesn't Work. You're Wrong.

How do you measure the effectiveness of an HR leader? I'll define HR leader fairly broadly to keep everyone engaged. Let's say that an HR leader is someone who not only leads the HR function for an entire company but is generally responsible over a client group of employees. If you support a line of business or a function and have a flock of employees to hire, train, and fire, you're an HR leader.

Talking about the effectiveness and performance of HR is a black hole. You've got the transactional side, performance, talent acquisition, etc. All subareas of HR have metrics, and HR leaders have been told that measurement is the key to the HR function being viewed as strategic.

But the top twenty metrics you can cite are really just white noise when it comes to measuring the effectiveness of an HR leader.

Revenue per employee (RPE) is the most important metric. Take the revenue produced by your company or business unit and divide it by your total number of employees to get RPE. Compare revenue per employee year over year for your HR leader. Did it go up or down? That's all you need to know. The rest is secondary and all of it just might be BS.

The naysayers tell me RPE is an imperfect measure, citing the need to measure profit and the fact that all revenue isn't good revenue. My response to both of those issues is pretty simple: an HR pro's contribution to profit is best measured by getting the most out of the people they have, and the denominator of the formula (per employee) is actually an expense number measured by FTEs. Lower revenue per employee means that you're likely delivering less potential profit to the company related to what you can control. Profit is present in the measurement based on the revenue/headcount dynamic. The side that says all revenue isn't good revenue? Try telling that to a wise CEO who wants higher revenue. The thought may be true (not all revenue is good revenue), but it's just noise and a reason to say no to the measurement. Start focusing on revenue per employee and let someone else figure out what's good and bad revenue. We're not qualified to determine that, and all that thinking does is cause paralysis by analysis.

10

Give Me What I Want or I'll Ruin Your Career (Assertiveness)

*I'm about to do to you what Limp Bizkit
did to music in the late '90s.*
—Wade Wilson (Ryan Reynolds) in *Deadpool* (2016)

When's the last time you blew up at somebody up at work? When's the last time someone blew up at you to hold you accountable or get what they wanted?

In either situation, the person doing the damage (you or the other person) might have a reputation for this type of thing. That type of reputation comes with a variety of tags depending on the personality, your company's culture, and how extreme the behavior is.

Need a list of the tags and identifiers? Try jackass for starters. There's also a variety of gender-related tags (both male and female) to describe aggressive behavior, but I'm a Midwestern kid and too nice to list them here.

Then there's the tag "assertive." This identifier is most often used to describe aggressive behavior in companies that use assessments and share profiles openly across teams, which is a cool practice but can lead to stereotypes and self-fulfilling prophecies. Here are two examples:

> Of course, Cheryl was going to destroy Bob on that project. She's so assertive, dude!
>
> Yeah, that conversation could have gone better—I shouldn't have made him cry. But I'm really assertive, and

it just kind of happens with me. (optional palms in the air and shoulder shrug)

Assertiveness is an interesting factor in the 9 Faces of HR model. Some profiles require a specific reading (low or high) as a primary characteristic of the persona while others treat the trait as secondary in nature.

But assertiveness is probably misunderstood in the world of HR. Let's dig in and see if we can get deeper than calling someone a jackass.

Let's Define Assertiveness as Something Other Than Being a Jackass

In researching this book, I was conflicted on how to define assertiveness.

Dictionary.com uses the following definition:

assertive—confidently aggressive or self-assured; positive: aggressive; dogmatic

But once you add the suffix to the word (-ness) and attempt to source a definition from organizations that specialize in the science of behavior, you get something a little different. Here's how *Psychology Today* defines "assertiveness":

assertiveness—the ability to formulate and communicate one's own thoughts, opinions and wishes in a clear, direct, and non-aggressive way.

Did you catch the difference? The world at-large includes "aggressive" in the definition, while the psychologists label assertiveness as "non-aggressive."

The truth probably lies somewhere in the middle, with both definitions illustrating a range of behaviors we could reasonably expect from a high assertive teammate.

One definition is a person hopeful for the world and workplace and cares what you think as whenever they are assertive with their opinions. In the other one, the assertive subject might have lit your car on fire to prove a point. You had it coming, because they tried the *Psychology Today* way and it didn't work out.

How to Spot a Low Assertive Teammate Without Really Trying

If you or someone you know answers yes to two or more of these questions, you're low assertive:

1. Are you a human doormat?
2. Has someone given you a t-shirt that says "human doormat"?
3. Do you say "yes" when you mean "no"?
4. Are you frightened by people in the sales department at your company?
5. Do you keep your opinions to yourself for fear of upsetting or starting an argument with others?
6. Do you refuse to tell others what you need from them, often at the risk of your own performance being viewed negatively?
7. Do you have a hard time bringing yourself to flag down a waiter proactively to get a refill? Do you wish they would just come over and do it?
8. Did you just sigh out loud?

HR's known as a service organization, so it can attract high performing, competent professionals who are low in the assertiveness dimension. If this is you, it's OK. You've done great work. As we'll see later when we get into the 9 Faces of HR, every team needs balance.

How to Spot a High Assertive Teammate
Without Really Trying

If you or someone you know answers yes to two or more of these questions, you're high assertive:

1. Have you changed the TV channel in your work break room when it was unclear if someone was actively watching what was currently playing?
2. Has someone ever called you a gender-related name (either male or female, or both) in response to your aggressive behavior in the workplace? These names might rhyme with Rick and ditch.
3. Have you ever told someone exactly what you thought in a meeting and witnessed people around you becoming physically uncomfortable?
4. Have you ever been told you have a habit of interrupting people?
5. When you want a refill, do you hold your glass in the air and start clinking your ice cubes around in the glass so your waiter understands your needs?
6. Have you ever made an offer on a car or a house that was so low your spouse was embarrassed?
7. Are you unsure what the big deal is after reading the items on this list?

Yeah, you're high assertive if you answer "yes" two or more times.

Who is Right? Does Assertiveness Include Aggression?

Everyone knows the No A**hole Rule.

A**holes are bad. A**holes are toxic. A**holes can ruin teams, lives, and—yes—the culture of your company if they are left unchecked.

I'm going to accept all of that and move on. A**holes suck.

But something happens to a lot of execs and HR pros who buy into the "No A**holes Rule." We flip the script and buy into what I'll call the *false negative on the No A**hole Rule*. That false negative goes like this:

> "If someone's not an a**hole, that means they're a good teammate and can be effective in our company."

That's not only inaccurate, it's dangerous.

The dirty little secret about difficult people who are highly assertive is that they get things done. Assertiveness, as it turns out, is necessary in our companies. We need people to push for results and accountability and to make others uncomfortable when either of those things are in short supply.

But overreacting to difficult people changes that. Once we have experience with a real jerk in the workplace, we automatically think that a skilled person who isn't assertive can be effective in a role that requires assertiveness.

The next time someone's pushing for a passive candidate who's great in every way but is being considered for a role that requires hard core assertiveness, take a pause and think.

No one wants to hire an a**hole, but properly displayed aggression with socially appropriate bumpers and respect for others is a reasonable part of any good definition of assertiveness.

Bonus

He's a Good Guy, Except for the Jihad

In HR, the intersection of assertiveness and processing speed can matter.

I was chilling out a few years back reading the *Wall Street Journal* (#humblebrag) and came across an article about how Belgian authorities had bungled an investigation that would have possibly prevented the Brussels terror attack.

Included in that bungling? A police interview that had a friend of one of the Brussels suicide bombers providing the following quote:

"He's a good guy, except for the Jihad."

Think about that quote for a second. Authorities in Belgium heard that quote and didn't take action that might have prevented the suicide attacks that subsequently occurred.

The rest of the world hears that quote, sees the lack of action, and gets fired up about the war on terror.

Me? I hear that quote and I'm reminded of the one thousand shades of gray of HR professionals trying to keep the peace and manage employee relations are faced with every week.

You and I know the reality. When you're in an HR position that includes heavy employee relations, you're going to get two hundred pieces of information a month that rise to the level of "disturbing." Some of those items about specific employees are work related, some are personal, and some are just stupid.

Still, you got the information. What are you going to do about it, HR? Generally, one of three things:

1. **Ignore it** because your BS filter tells you it's not real
2. **Put it on the watch list or in the memory bank** because it's problematic but not life-threatening right now
3. **Take action ASAP** because what might happen if you ignore it is something you and the company can't live with

For most of us in HR, clear examples of option three (take action ASAP) include risks related to workplace violence, harassment, etc.

Still, at times we get caught telling ourselves that we don't have to take action on bad stuff coming across our desk. Why is that? The following qualifiers tell us we have time:

» **We got the information from a third party of questionable credibility.** You know this one—the source isn't great and to truly investigate, you might have to blow the doors off of someone you like. So, you put it on the watch list and hope it doesn't blow up in your face.

» **We rationalize that the target of the bad stuff in our organization is a less than stellar player and might have brought it on themselves.** Translation—we don't like them and neither does the company, so we're slower to act. The watch list is a perfect solution for this circumstance.

» **The information we were given is too general.** Do we really know there's a problem? We rationalize that information is directional in nature, and we pledge to keep our eyes on it.

» **We're busy, dammit.** Yep, we only have so much cycle time, and if the information provided is foggy at best, it doesn't rise to the level of digging in and launching a more formal investigation.

HR people doing employee relations have a lot in common with the FBI trying to make sense of bad stuff happening. There's data coming across your screen, you can't trust most people to avoid putting their own spin on a given situation, and you're understaffed.

As a result, it's up to you to decide when you need to launch a formal investigation and start getting to the bottom of reported bad stuff at play in your organization.

"He's a good guy, except for the Jihad."

Replace Jihad with something less threatening, and you have your life in HR.

"He's a good guy, except for the way he acts around women."

Good luck with people coming at you this week to report bad stuff. Your job in HR requires you to make quick decisions on who's credible and who's not. High cognitive skills and processing speed means you're better than most in deciding what's real and what's not. High assertiveness means you don't blink and avoid going after things you need to go after.

If you're good at this, you've got nothing to worry about.

If you're not? You probably need to spend more of your time doing formal investigations to make sure the bad stuff doesn't hurt you—or your company.

11

Take this OPS Manual and Shove It (Rules Orientation)

Badges? We don't need no stinking badges.
—Bandit in *Blazing Saddles* (1974)

Let's Define Rules Orientation because That's What a High Rules Person Would Do

Does your employee need the operations manual to thrive at your company or would they rather wing it?

It's a more important question than you might think, and it's related to an area I call "Rules Orientation." Rules Orientation measures whether a candidate or employee seeks change or stability, needs rules to cope with the world around them, or has the ability to adapt to situations on the fly.

Almost every behavioral assessment on the market will have its version of Rules Orientation, although it might be named differently. Read the descriptions, it's there.

Since part of the 9 Faces of HR model measures the ability to innovate, drive change, and add value, Rules Orientation is a key part of this book. Being high rules or low rules isn't good or bad. Context is key because certain positions and activities in the world of HR demand structure related to policy, process, and transactions. Other HR positions have to figure things out on the fly in chaotic environments. Many HR jobs exist somewhere in the middle.

HR pros who exist at the extremes of Rules Orientation (high and low) have different needs. If you mismatch them to the opportunity in question, you'll have turnover within a year. Making the right match related to Rules Orientation requires you to look at the amount of structure that exists within the HR job in question, your company culture, and the team/boss match.

If you build your HR team without thinking about Rules Orientation, you're asking for a dumpster fire.

How to Spot a Low Rules Teammate Without Really Trying

Low rules people are change junkies.

Low rules people are down with the sickness—they love that freak show you call a company. Having no set plan to deal with what they're encountering doesn't bother them. They'd rather be in control of what they decide to do in any given situation.

Low rules people have a name for chaos. They call it "Tuesday."

You can ask a low rules person to help you build the operations manual that the high rules people need for your growing company. They'll enjoy that process because they are creating order from chaos but be prepared—they'll be ready to bolt as soon as you start holding them accountable to following the manual. It doesn't matter that they wrote it, they need change.

You might be a low rules person if:

1. You change offices in your building every six months because you get bored being in the same place.
2. You're not satisfied at work unless you're chasing a new project you find interesting.
3. You like talking about new ideas and actually believe the saying that "there are no bad ideas in brainstorming."
4. You "pity the fools" who have to do the same thing day in, day out.

5. You took responsibility for stocking the snack machine just so you could change the positions of the biggest selling items (Snickers and M&Ms) monthly. You love messing with the lemmings.

You can't have a company of nothing but low rules people. But one without them doesn't work either.

The problem is that your company most likely can't provide an environment where the low-rules HR pro can be successful. You can want it, but you'll likely still fail when hiring a low-rules HR person.

A low-rules HR pro joining a high-red tape company leads to frustrations from the level of approval that would be necessary to get things done and drive change. It will be tough for them to be successful (often in their own eyes) because of the time it takes to push a great idea through the change process.

How to Spot a High Rules Teammate Without Really Trying

High rules people dig structure. If you're a freak show of a company, be careful. The high rules candidate belongs at a utility, or in a position where it's all mapped out.

To be fair, being high rules doesn't mean a person is not smart and talented. Being high rules simply means you like to operate within structure and understand expectations before you apply your significant talents.

HR as a function is known to provide a "safe haven" for high rules people through the following activities:

1. Doing payroll
2. Forms, Forms, Forms (sung to the tune of Motley Crue's "Girls, Girls, Girls")
3. Enforcing a policy that clearly states a company's position on "X"

4. Policing appropriate use of yoga pants in relationship to dress code policy (spoiler alert—there is no appropriate use of yoga pants at work, suckers!)

5. Saying no to wayward souls who don't understand that policies are black and white

6. Finding the gal who keeps changing the location of Snickers and M&Ms in the snack machine

Other functions in corporate America that high rules people find attractive: accounting, compliance, and quality assurance.

Implications of Rules Orientation in the World of HR

I've said it once in this section, and I'm going to say it again: you need a mix of low- and high-rules people on an HR team of any size.

That being said, high-rules people in HR are routinely easy to find. The history of the work draws people who want structure for all the aforementioned reasons. HR generally does not have enough low rules people in the function's team mix.

When big HR functions get stuck, the high-end consultants come in and sell bulky competency models that look great in the roll-out meeting and then don't get used by anyone. That's as true for HR competency models as it is for any other functional area.

So I'm going to give you the three HR competencies that truly matter. The rest might be nice, but they aren't at the core to what makes a great HR manager/director/business resource partner (HRBP) level. Here's what I've got that's critical for your HR function, with some notes on how recruiting low rules HR people might need to be part of your plan:

1. **Ability to Negotiate.** This covers a lot of ground, but an HR pro's ability to read the situation, see what's possible, and negotiate for the company, HR as a unit, and for themselves

is crucial to the outcomes you'll get. Do you have HR pros willing and able to use the same sales tactics as a high-level sales pro? Then you have a big element to what you need as an HR function.

2. **Innovation.** Innovation is a strong word and a buzzword most of the time, so let's dumb it down. What innovation means from an HR pro is *whether they can create a work product that wows the people they serve and have it packaged in a way where the marketing of the idea takes care of itself.* Example? You need an executive comp analysis done but don't have the budget. Can your HR pro go find resources (beg, borrow, or steal) to create something and present it in a way where everyone has faith in the product? Or is she simply asking for money for outside consultants to do it? Low rules people understand "beg, borrow, and steal." High rules people want to pay someone to do it.

3. **Says "Yes" more than they say "No."** This will give many a cause for pause, but let's face it: the HR pros who the rest of the business world don't respect are the ones who say "no" all the time. The HR pros with the right stuff listen and find ways to say "yes" with conditions (work needed from the requestor to make the "yes" a reality). HR pros at all levels who aren't viewed as players say "no" more than they say "yes." This is tied to rules orientation.

I think these three HR competencies are tied to rules orientation to some extent. The HR pros who can do these three things are worth their weight in gold.

All other HR competencies? Meh.

How Elon Musk Decided if His Assistant Needed a Raise

Speaking of **Rules Orientation**, it's notable that your boss's worldview (as well as that of the business leaders you support in HR) is as important as your own in this area.

Bosses write the rules. We react to bosses.

Case in point? Elon Musk, founder and CEO of Tesla and SpaceX.

Low Rules Bosses Are Fun!

Elon Musk is one of the most interesting CEOs in the world. He's also one of the most independent. How do you manage a boss with similar characteristics?

You don't. Just like you don't control a cat, you don't manage the independent, low rules boss.

In his 2015 book *Elon Musk: Tesla, SpaceX, and the Quest for a Fantastic Future*, Ashlee Vance shares the story of how Musk stopped working with his longtime executive assistant in early 2014.

According to Vance, Mary Beth Brown, the assistant, asked Musk for a significant raise after she'd been working with him for twelve years. In response, Musk told Brown to take two weeks off, during which he would assume her responsibilities and see whether she was critical to his success. When Brown returned, Musk told her he didn't need her anymore. Whoops!

While Musk generally is on the record as saying this book is accurate, he strongly denies the reporting of this encounter. Brown also denies the reporting that she lost her job through the comical efficiency study conducted by Musk. Also, after Brown was no longer in the role, Musk says he needed the position, as evidenced by the fact he hired two to three specialists (PR, etc.) rather than a generalist executive assistant.

> You know, Mary Beth, I've been thinking. You're great, but what would the world look like if I reorganized and hired three people to do your job?

Still, where there's smoke, there's fire. My take is that Musk probably did thoughtfully consider whether the position still worked for him based on the way his business has changed.

Add this to the reasons to be careful asking the low rules boss for anything. The most common error employees make with a low rules boss is taking an offer to their boss expecting a counteroffer. Rather than countering, the tough, unpredictable boss wishes the employee luck in the new position.

Want a raise? Interesting. How about you take a couple of days off while I determine how vital you are to the organization?

Goal Settting and the Visionary Low Rules Boss

In addition to allegedly terminating assistants in an abrupt fashion, Musk is a pretty extreme goal setter, using the Big, Hairy, Audacious Goal setting technique (BHAG).

BHAGs are visionary strategy statements designed to focus a group of people around a common initiative. They differ from our other goal setting techniques because BHAGS are **set forth by a large group** (rather than individuals) and **typically span a larger amount of time** than any of our other goals. They're huge.

BHAGs can come in several flavors. Most are focused on one of four broad categories: reaching a defined target or metric, competition, organizational change, or reputation. Here are a few BHAG examples from some companies about which you might have heard:

» **Reaching a defined target**
   "Attain 1 billion customers worldwide"—Citicorp, 1990s

» **Competition**
   "Crush Adidas"—Nike, 1960s

» **Organizational Change**
   "Transform this company from a chemical manufacturer into one of the preeminent drug-making companies in the world."—Merck, 1930s

» **Reputation**
   "Become the company most known for changing the world-wide poor-quality image of Japanese products"—Sony, 1950s

Wait—Nike wasn't always the leader? Japanese products were once considered low quality before Japan was kicking the USA's a** in the 1980s?

Before the world as we know it, leaders at those companies created a BHAG as a single, unified vision for their people to rally around.

Musk basically BHAG'd his way into Tesla and Space X becoming great companies from nothing. Electric car with quality and luxury (Tesla)? BHAG. Reusable rockets with segments that can land back on earth on landing pads (SpaceX)? B-freaking-HAG.

Well, here comes Musk again, probably the most adept user of BHAGs in the world. The topic is Mars—more from *The Guardian*:

> Elon Musk has unveiled plans for a new spacecraft that he says would allow his company SpaceX to colonize Mars, build a base on the moon, and allow commercial travel to anywhere on Earth in under an hour. The spacecraft is

currently still codenamed the BFR. Musk says the company hopes to have the first launch by 2022, and then have four flying to Mars by 2024.

Last year Musk proposed an earlier plan for the spacecraft, but at the time had not developed a way of funding the project. Speaking at the International Astronautical Congress in Adelaide Australia on Friday, Musk said the company had figured out a way to pay for the project.

The key, he said, was to "cannibalise" all of SpaceX's other products. Instead of operating a number of smaller spacecrafts to deliver satellites into orbit and supply the International Space Station, Musk said the BFR would eventually be used to complete all of its missions. "If we can do that then all the resources that are used for Falcon9, Dragon and Heavy can be applied to this system," he said.

BFR. Musk isn't messing around. Let's go to Mars. The BHAG is set.

If history tells us nothing else, it tells us that Musk will probably make it happen. Maybe not by 2024, but you can't have a BHAG without making it seem impossible.

Remember to Take the Microphone Away from the Low Rules Boss

2018 was rough in many ways for the public persona of Elon Musk.

First, in a tweet, he floated an idea for taking Tesla private for $420 per share and settled securities fraud charges as a result. Then he had Azealia Banks, a female rapper, over to one of his homes. Banks started live tweeting a bunch of stuff that was unflattering and accused him of light investment fraud, among other things. To top it off, he smoked weed live on podcaster Joe Rogan's show.

But you know what's going well for Musk? Embarrassing employees who are jumping to Apple by tagging them all a certain way. He spoke to the German newspaper Handelsbatt in 2015, stating **"We always jokingly call Apple the 'Tesla Graveyard.' If you don't make it at Tesla, you go work at Apple. I'm not kidding."**

Various reports in 2018 reported Apple was on a hiring spree, poaching "scores" of ex-Tesla employees for a variety of projects, citing better pay at the iPhone giant. The companies are infamous for trading development and design talent.

If Tesla was doing an employer value proposition (EVP) study, two of the themes would undoubtedly be "we work on the bleeding edge" and "everyone here is all in."

Low rules and no filter bosses have a tough time not saying what they think. Part of this radical candor is framing defections to a world class competitor for talent as the "lazy people" or people who were "not good enough to work here."

Love it or hate it, it's an aggressive approach you can learn from. Our body language and framing when people leave our companies tends to be too passive.

Elon Musk. The most interesting man in the world—and a low rules boss that someone in HR has to figure out and react to.

12

May I Show You My Signed Picture of Dale Carnegie? (Detail Orientation)

I can't stop calling the OCD hotline.
—Kent Graham

My company gets the opportunity to be involved in thousands of hires every year. It's an interesting test tube, especially since we help other companies hire great talent. So, it's not *our* culture we're hiring for most of the time, but the individual cultures of the clients who partner with Kinetix.

As part of that, I've grown up a little bit when it comes to assessments. Growing up is healthy. I encourage everyone to give it a shot.

What have I learned about the behavioral traits of candidates? Plenty. Let me give you some notes related to a very important trait that most assessment platforms cover: Detail Orientation.

Let's Define Detail Orientation So You Can Cross It Off Your List, Freak

Detail Orientation outlines how organized an individual is, whether they react to or plan for events, how they manage time, what their project management skills are, etc. Clipboards, lists, and color-coding are the earmarks of someone who has a **High Details** score. They're punctual and have a strong eye for details. These are the folks you want reviewing the presentation before it's sent out to the client. A Low Details score means that someone is not going to lead your company in to-do list completion. If you're expecting meticulous planning and organizing from this person, you are way off base.

How Detail Orientation Influences The 9 Faces of HR Model

High Details Orientation is generally a feature of the personas with a lower ability to innovate, drive change, and add value in the 9 Faces of HR. When combined with high rules orientation, it creates a powerful combination of command and control HR.

Personas within the 9 Faces of HR model with mid- to high-range ability to innovate, drive change, and add value display higher variability when it comes to Rules Orientation. Detail orientation in these personas is considered a strength until it reaches the 90th percentile and above, at which point the need for order may override other behavioral dimensions.

How to Spot a Low Details Teammate Without Really Trying

People who are low details (I'm just below the mean) are not list builders. They are less organized than high detail people. Tasks can slide from day to day and from week to week and they sleep like a baby—they're not bothered. The high details person can't take that.

How you know you're dealing with a low details person:

1. They forgot they were scheduled to meet with you.
2. They like to call themselves a "big picture" thinker.
3. When you ride them in a way that indicates you value details over anything else, they get this little smirk on their face that makes you want to smack them.

4. They seem to have nine lives related to their lack of details. People keep bailing them out because of their value in other areas.

5. They just asked you if you've seen their keys.

How to Spot a High Details Teammate Without Really Trying

People who are high details are list builders, and they have a list to guide them every day. They have coded priorities in the list, and they get stressed if they are not in a position to cross things off the list.

How you know you're dealing with a high details person:

1. They ask questions. No, I mean they ask a LOT of questions.

2. After a meeting, they're the ones sending out the summary of the minutes and the subsequent "to-do" list.

3. They're freaking out because there's not what they are calling "a plan."

4. Your interviewing team meets to interview candidates and make a decision on who to hire. The rest of the team is clear—candidate B is best. The high details person can't get past a punctuation error on the resume, so they vote "no" on candidate B even though they acknowledge she was the best candidate in other ways.

5. They found your keys before you knew they were missing.

HR Teams Need Detail Orientation, But Can't Value It Above Everything Else

As a function with a deep history in process, policy, and transactions, HR has a clear need for detail orientation. This fact is not in question, but how much weight detail orientation has compared to other behavioral dimensions is something smart HR leaders should debate.

Things need to be ordered. Things need to be correct and executed without errors.

The danger for HR leaders everywhere is whether they consider detail orientation (as well as rules orientation) to be the primary value of their HR function or merely a feature that supports the deeper strategic competencies being pursued.

How Low and High Details People Drive Each Other Crazy on HR Teams

It takes a village to put good HR service out the door, which means the smart HR leader won't value detail orientation over all else. That means most modern HR teams will have team members across the detail orientation spectrum.

Here are five things I've learned about detail orientation in my career that should guide how you build your HR team:

1. **On a team of any size, you need high details people to get s*** done.** Let's say you're a maverick HR leader—you are what we'll define later in this book as "The Natural," which means you're in your role with an eye on innovation and change. Your first instinct will be to hire people who are like you at all levels because to drive the change, your team has to be the change (shout out to change agent Mahatma Gandhi). But if all you hire are change agents, you're likely to end up with less detail orientation in your function than you need to survive. Things won't get done. Do yourself a favor—hire some people with the detail orientation necessary to make your dreams a reality.

2. **Low details people will drive high details people crazy. Crazy, I say.** There's a natural conflict with low and high details people. Unfortunately for them, the super high details crowd can have a form of details OCD, which means the low details people are going to drive them completely insane. But the low details people are likely viewed as high performers for strengths in other areas, so they're not going anywhere.

3. **High details people don't generally drive low details people crazy.** Low details FTEs think the high details people are adorable when they're freaking out. The casual reactions and body language (as well as the aforementioned smirks) emulated by the low detail people when being taken to task on organizational skills only serve to drive the high details people bonkers.

4. **If allowed to, high details people will create a culture where crossing things off a list trumps the value of creativity and ideas.** Turns out you need both. Balance is the key. The history of HR is in rules and process, so it's easy for traditional personas to rule the day in HR. The faster the pace of change in the world, the more innovation and change management skills are at a premium in the world of HR.

5. **One of the most powerful combinations in today's business world is Low Rules Orientation, High Detail Orientation.** This combination means someone likes the chaos of an unstructured situation and wants to create the solution (creativity and idea generation comes with that) but has the detail orientation necessary to get the ideas organized and execute on the plan.

The greatest trick the devil ever played was convincing us that diversity is solely defined by Title VII definitions. Just as important as the normal definition of diversity is making sure you don't surround yourself with mini-me's—carbon copies from a behavioral perspective.

Never assume your behavioral profile is the right one.

Unless your profile looks like mine. Then you're perfect.

13

Let's Do This: A Tour of the 9 Faces of HR

*After a while, you learn to ignore the names
people call you and just trust who you are.*
—Shrek

Now that we've had a chance to dig in and understand how the 9 Faces of HR model works (a 9-box grid with "HR career level" on the first axis and "ability to innovate, drive change, and add value" on the second axis), it's time to introduce you to the faces and personas that make up the world of HR. Are you ready? Of course you are.

The most interesting thing related to the 9 Faces of HR is to think about which persona is uniquely yours. The second most interesting thing is to think about which of the faces the people you love (and hate) in the world of HR are. You're going to read the next nine chapters and say, "I know that hero" (usually your persona) or "I know that jackass!" (the persona of someone you can't stand).

With that in mind, here are a few ground rules to keep you sane as you start digging into the 9 Faces of HR:

1. **There's no such thing as a "good face" or a "bad face" in the 9 Faces of HR.** It all comes down to fit. HR shops in big *Fortune* 500 environments need all 9 Faces to effectively deliver HR services. While some might think the more controlling personas (you'll meet the Judge and the Cop soon) are non-desirable, the reality is that these personas are

necessary on large HR teams and can also be the most effective persona in some smaller companies as well. It all depends on the environment and the expectations of the organization in question—there's no bad persona, only bad fits with the organization they serve.

2. **Evaluating HR career level is not always title driven.** Some of you hold director and VP of HR titles and are going to automatically place yourself at the senior level. The reality is more nuanced—big titles in smaller organizations are often mid-career level within the 9 Faces of HR model. Be honest about the scope of your position—if you couldn't get a job at a much larger company with that director or VP-level title, odds are you're mid-career when it comes to The 9 Faces of HR. There's nothing wrong with that!

3. **Ability to innovate, drive change, and add value is not absolute. Gray areas are present.** There are Fixers who are really close to being Assassins and Mentors who are two domineering emails away from being Judges. If I put you through my assessment package, you're rarely going to be dead center for the persona for which you're ultimately identified as. Some of you will see yourself in multiple personas and faces related to the ability to innovate and drive change, and that is 100 percent normal.

4. **The biggest benefit you receive when evaluating yourself with the 9 Faces of HR model is self-awareness.** The world is changing for HR pros everywhere, as noted in the first chapter with Jenn from GridLoad. Staying ahead has a lot to do with self-awareness and understanding who you are as well as the signals you're sending out during times of change.

As you dig into the individual profiles of the 9 Faces of HR in the following chapters, I'll encourage you with three words: find your fit. Regardless of your persona within the 9 Faces of HR, there's a company, boss, and environment that is right for you.

Some of you are reading this book and experiencing waves of change at work and might even be confused as to why you aren't being valued more than you are. I get it and want to help you survive that. You've got a mortgage—perhaps a kid or two— and need to keep getting paid.

The pain that comes with widespread change is a threat for all of us in today's business world. Self-awareness is key, and by understanding your natural state in the 9 Faces of HR, you'll maximize yourself in your current company and, if needed, have a better understanding of what you're looking for if you seek another gig.

Enjoy the stories that follow.

14

The Natural

I feel like I'm too busy writing history to read it.
—Kayne West

Most professions have larger-than-life leaders at the top of the job pyramid. "Larger-than-life" refers to rock-star status because CEOs and top SVPs of functional areas like marketing and engineering generally maintain high profiles in the world outside your company.

HR also has rock stars. But top HR leaders are often like the wind: here one moment and gone the next. We call this rare shooting-star leader profile "the Natural."

It Was Time for Roger to Fly

Roger looked down at his phone and saw the number as he left the benefits planning session. They were back, just like they said they'd be back. As the Chief People Officer at HeartSpark, Roger had parachuted in with the new leadership team four years ago, put in place by the private equity (PE) firm of record. At the time he joined, HeartSpark had five hundred employees, but growth in the healthcare technology startup had been strong, and the company now had 3,500 full-time employees.

Figure 14.1. Roger, the Natural

Roger was widely known as the architect of the HeartSpark culture, but just as importantly, he had built a human capital machine, creating a widely recognized recruiting function as well as a world-class platform across the entire HR function. He was especially proud of the equity plan he had designed and tweaked over time as it had created something he called "organization gravity," which meant industry-leading retention.

Roger looked at the transcript of the voicemail as he walked back to his office. The message was short but sweet—the headhunter was informing him the software company was back with a new offer for the VP of product management role they had approached him with three months ago. The new offer represented a 30 percent increase in base salary and kept him whole in bonus and incentive compensation.

For Roger, moving wasn't about the money. It was about being flat. Did he really want to sit through another meeting discussing how they could remain cost neutral against rising healthcare costs by tweaking co-pays?

As Roger walked to his office, he thought about life in product management for a software company doing cool things in the compensation space. It seemed fresh and in line with what he wanted for a next step. HeartSpark had been great, as had pure play HR—but four years was a long time.

Roger is the Natural in the 9 Faces of HR model.

As his feet left the ground and he landed in his chair, Roger hit the "call-back" button on the voicemail.

It was time for Roger to fly.

Who Is the Natural in the 9 Faces of HR?

The Natural is at the top of the food chain in the 9 Faces of HR model, located in the top right in our 9-box grid. That means individuals who fit into the Natural profile are senior-level HR Leaders with maximum ability to innovate, drive change, and add value in their organizations.

While Naturals of the HR world can rise from the ranks, they are rare birds in the world of human capital. Our experience estimates that less than one percent of the HR world fits into this persona, significantly lower than the other personas present at the senior level—the Judge and the Mentor.

Things to know about the Naturals of HR:

» They are routinely viewed as creators and innovators.
» They are good at incubating culture inside organizations.
» HR teams reporting to the Natural respect them as visionary but at times wish they were more connected to the day-to-day work.
» They are highly curious about the world around them.
» At their core, they don't view themselves as HR pros.
» They are better marketers than any of their peers in the HR world.

It's easy to love a Natural as the leader of your HR function. Love them now because they may not be around next month. They've got options that transcend our function.

Let's Check the DNA of the Natural, Shall We?

You might think by looking at the grid of the 9 Faces of HR that the Natural is simply the senior, more experienced version of the Assassin. You're partially right, but the Naturals of the world have one tweak that allows them to ascend to and thrive in HR Leadership roles. Let's dig in.

Primary DNA Characteristics of a the Natural

» **High Cognitive/High Processing Speed.** Like the Assassin, the Natural has an incredible ability to take in large amounts of data and make quick and accurate decisions. You generally won't find a Natural who is not in the top 10 percent of cognitive ability compared to the general population.

This horsepower allows the Natural to be curious about all things related to the business and the world around them. Curiosity naturally blends into making connections about what's possible for the HR function within a specific company. In this fashion, the Naturals are like high-end consultants—they see a need and they create a solution better than the rest of their senior-level peers.

» **Very Low Rules Orientation.** To have clear eyes and a full heart related to change, it's necessary for a Natural to score in the lowest quartile related to rules orientation. Being low rules is critical to the Natural's consultant-based mind and delivering big change where others can't see the opportunity or craft the solution.

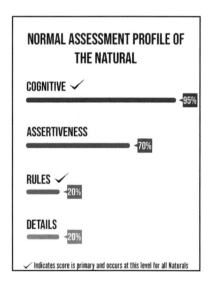

Figure 14.2. Scorecard for the Natural

Secondary DNA Characteristics of a the Natural

» **Mid to High Assertiveness.** Unlike the Assassin, the Natural doesn't have to have top quartile assertiveness. Simply being at mid-level assertiveness is enough to keep the wolves at bay as part of the leadership team. While the Assassin can be a "bull in a china shop" when it comes to taking action, the more nuanced approach of the Natural is more befitting of a visionary leader. Plus, that's why the Natural has Assassins, right?

» **Detail Orientation.** Simply put, the Natural has people to manage the details. Vision is the currency of this leader. It's most common for them to reside in the low- to mid-level of detail orientation.

The Natural is just like you and me. Except they see things that we can't, which is why they are in the top-right box.

Where Does the Natural Come From?

The Natural is the least likely of the three senior-level personas in our model to rise from the HR ranks to lead your HR function. Simply put, what the Natural is good at isn't necessarily valued in early- to mid-career HR roles. Where does the Natural come from? Here are some thoughts:

» **Rotational programs.** As mentioned earlier in this book, big companies have rotational programs for high-potential employees (HIPOs) as part of succession strategies, and HR is often a part of that rotation. From time to time, HIPOs are rotated into HR, love it, are highly effective, and never leave or they come back to HR after their rotations are complete. In other circumstances, high performers are parachuted into HR on an interim basis to put out a burning dumpster fire, find their perfect match, and stay for the good times. If a senior-level HIPO with behavioral characteristics that match the profile is rotated into HR, a Natural can be born.

» **As a strategic play to move an HR team from transactional focus.** It's not uncommon for a new leader to come into your company and view the HR function as lacking in strategy and being too focused on transactions. Regardless if that analysis is accurate, the prescribed antidote is often hiring a new HR leader. Non-traditional hires are often made in response to the stated need—enter the Natural.

» **An Assassin who exists in your company with manageable assertiveness.** While Assassins generally have a shelf life of two years at any company, at times you'll find them with just the right amount of assertiveness—high enough to be coded as an Assassin, but low enough to qualify as the Natural once the experience and knowledge is high enough to be viewed as senior level. If this person can survive in mid-career HR at your company, ultimately, they'll have the DNA to become your Natural.

It's hard to find a the Natural to lead your HR function. If you have one, it likely happened through the perfect mix of career arc, opportunity and of course, luck.

Why Does the Natural Leave Your Company and Where Do They Go?

Like our buddy Roger at the start of this chapter, HR Leaders who fit the Natural vibe are probably not going to be your HR leader for the next ten years. There are simply too many market forces at work. They're a curious type, with the possibility of greater intellectual challenge on the other side of the street always in play.

In addition to curiosity, there's also one HR-centric issue at play which may drive them from pure play, corporate HR: *HR has a command-and-control element that is necessary at times. HR has transactions that need to get done and must be valued in any HR function. The Natural doesn't find either of these realities particularly compelling.*

The Natural is about vision, purpose, and a sense of transformation contribution. They find your payroll ledger and policy manuals boring—even pedestrian. That reality means that the Natural is likely to bounce outside of the world of HR for their next gig. Common landing spots for their next gig include the following:

» **Another functional area (marketing, anyone?).** The Natural likely has borrowed principles from other functional areas as part of their approach to HR. To the extent they went deep undercover in their research, they may have acquired enough knowledge to be dangerous in an area like marketing.

Now imagine your CEO thinks the Natural is a HIPO. One day, your marketing leader says she's tired of everyone's s*** and walks out. The Natural throws their name in the hat for that job, and they're also running the search personally. What do you think is going to happen?

» **A consulting firm in the human capital space.** If there's one thing that the Natural is good at, it's thinking about solutions. Moving to a consulting firm fits, but unless your Natural has experience in sales, it likely needs to be a big shop where they can do delivery only.

» **Vendors in the human capital space.** Like our buddy Roger, the Natural profile makes for a great vendor hire. Think about it—the Natural has deep subject matter experience and likely has a positive disposition towards technology.

» **A company that's cooler than yours.** Maybe even smaller. Sometimes the Natural doesn't make a choice to exit the profession. In this circumstance, they get an HR leadership position with another, cooler firm where they can think transformational thoughts. Sometimes they go smaller because the challenges are "purer" than in that sausage machine you call a company.

The Natural doesn't think they are above you. They feel your pain and would love to lead you and the team to a better place. Until they are needed elsewhere. Then the Natural will give you the news (they're leaving), say something cool about your potential, and note that their Uber Black is about to pull up.

They are out.

Bonus

We're All Working for the Same Boss, Aren't We?

It's hard to think about the real-life Naturals without smiling. They seem to bring more than work to the table. Truth and love as supreme values. The clothing on brand, the sense of grace. The Natural brings people from different backgrounds together naturally. But for the rest of us common folk (you and me), sometimes religion gets in the way.

It was Ash Wednesday, people. Time for Christians everywhere to give something up for Lent. Or the heart of Mardi Gras season—I guess it depends on your disposition.

I've seen one epic fail related to religion in the workplace in my time as an HR pro. The year was 2003, and I was a VP of HR at a big telecom. We had a great peer group of HR leaders nationally, and we were in St. Louis for a quarterly meeting.

Brain trust time. Bonding. And one of the meeting days fell on Ash Wednesday.

Ten HR leaders for a *Fortune* 500 telecom traveled to St. Louis—two guys and eight gals. As you might expect, the gals were more in tune with fashion and personal appearance, especially as it related to each other. Me? Blue shirt, black slacks. Check.

But our female HR leaders had more diversity in their appearance, and as any group that works together well would do, they talked to each other about clothes, fashion, etc.

Then it happened on Ash Wednesday. One female HR leader of the Catholic faith made her way out to church during lunch and came back with the mark of the cross from ashes on her forehead.

Enter her VP of HR teammate, whom I'll call "Tonya." Tonya was Baptist. She was also one of the best HR leaders I have ever known, but on that day, she would take two steps back as a teammate to her Catholic friend, known here as "Susan."

Susan had the mark of the cross on her forehead and it must have been made by a pastor with fat thumbs, because it didn't look like a cross—it looked like a thumbprint. But wear it with pride she did, back into the national HR meetings.

Tonya didn't know much about Ash Wednesday, and subsequently I learned that many Baptists don't practice Lent.

Anyway, Susan turned the corner back into the meeting room with the ashes on her forehead, and Tonya beat a quick path to her to be helpful, uttering the following words:

> Susan—You've got a smudge on your forehead. Let me
> help you.

And with that, she wetted her thumb and started trying to remove the ashes from Susan's forehead.

Astonishment, borderline anger, and general confusion ensued. It was one of the more surreal religious workplace interactions I've seen in the workplace.

I like to think the Natural could have calmed everyone down with something like:

> You know Susan, greatness, self-sacrifice, and generosity
> are the exclusive possession of no one race or religion.
> Also, you still have a little smudge. I say let's leave it!

Naturals just always know what to say in tough situations. That's why they're Naturals.

15

The Mentor

*A mentor is someone who allows you
to see the hope inside yourself.*
—Oprah Winfrey

*I am out here for you. You don't know what
it's like to be ME out here for YOU. It is
an up-at-dawn, pride-swallowing siege that
I will never fully tell you about, okay?*
—Jerry McGuire (Tom Cruise) in *Jerry McGuire* (1996)

Meet Jill, The Mentor

"I'm SO tired."

It wasn't rare for this thought to slip into Jill's mind during any given week. But it was Tuesday, and the thought came earlier this week than most.

Jill was the chief human resource officer (CHRO) at GroceryRunner.com. As a 43-year-old career-minded HR pro, she had climbed the corporate ladder quicker than most. The first twenty years of her career were spent at a variety of brands most of her peers

Figure 15.1. Jill the Mentor

recognized: GE, Chase, and, most recently, Amazon. She had built a career as an HR business partner—long on advice and counsel, short on BS. The business people she had served at all stops trusted her.

But GroceryRunner was different. She viewed the grocery shopping service—which had grown to 3,000 employees in five years—to be the perfect first stop as a CHRO. Headhunters always called, but when Korn Ferry called her with this opportunity two years ago, she felt it was ideal for her. E-commerce and logistics? Her five years at Amazon had prepared her well, and she made the decision to accept the offer the day after her husband threw her a surprise party for her fortieth birthday.

Six months after she joined GroceryRunner, Amazon announced their acquisition of Whole Foods.

Her former boss at Amazon reached out to her the morning the deal was announced. She almost threw up when she read his text.

Now GroceryRunner was in a fight for its life. They were in year four of their current private equity round, and fear, doubt, and uncertainty ruled the day. Nowhere was this more apparent than in the myopic, short-term view and behavior of the leadership team and their direct reports.

Jill looked at the list of projects her HR team was attempting to deliver as she walked down the hallway. She was proud of the team she had built in three years. They were deeply talented, and she had encouraged them to stretch and help her build an HR practice unlike any other.

Of the seven big initiatives they were chasing, Jill counted five that were in trouble—two due to her direct reports failing as they stretched, and three in peril as business leaders claimed they didn't have time for what they termed "non-essential activities."

As Jill entered the conference room for the weekly LT meeting, she braced herself for battle. She knew two of her nine peers would be actively critical. She had already reached out to three neutral parties to ensure their support during the weekly free-for-all.

It wasn't her first rodeo. If she didn't represent, no one would.

What It's Like to Work for The Mentor

Jill is the Mentor in the 9 Faces of HR model.

Some of you think you are working for a Mentor today. Many of you are reporting a false positive version of this desired leadership profile.

What do I mean by false positive? The Mentor is more than a supportive boss or a shoulder to cry on. The Mentor is a senior-level HR Leader with mid-range ability to innovate, drive change, and add value. This mid-range ability is important, because it means they are comfortable with a wide range of direct reports.

True matches to the Mentor persona care how you feel, but if you're not extremely talented, they care much less. They're not here to raise children, they're here to win. It just so happens that their model to win includes a bunch of professional development for those who report to them.

If you're lucky enough to get hired by a Mentor like Jill, here's what you can expect:

1. **The Mentor will figure out what makes you tick and develop a personal coaching model for you.** That's right. The Mentor actually cares about what makes you different and wants to consider that in their interactions with you. Sometimes they really care about you. Sometimes they don't. The key is that they understand that great people can do great work if they understand the motivations of others. You win either way because even if they're looking right through you in your one-on-one, their focus on your needs makes you feel warm inside. The Mentor will say something that makes you feel like the most important person in the world every time you spend thirty minutes with them. #mindgames

2. **The Mentor will encourage and expect you to chase big wins.** The Mentor takes their desire to be known as the internal agent for stars very seriously. They know you won't get a

reputation as a rising HR star by being "good with the process side." With that in mind, you're going to be expected to chase some big wins.

What's a big win? A big win is a project that has impact on a functional area other than HR. Maybe you should redesign sales comp in conjunction with the EVP of sales. Perhaps you could figure out a way to cut 10 percent of the workforce with no drop in production or efficiency. Look around and find a potential big win—actually, make that two or three big wins. The Mentor is going to expect you to have star power. Working for the Mentor is not for the sleepy side of HR.

3. **The Mentor is not going to tell you how to do your job. But they do expect to be updated.** Even if the Mentor brainstorms big wins with you or assigns you one, don't wait around for them to develop the project plan for you. As Don Draper once said on Mad Men—"That's what the money is for." The Mentor expects their direct reports (and even those two notches below them on the organizational chart) to have the chops to deliver on project work once identified. You said you wanted to be developed. Make sure your definition matches theirs. You just wanted to go get drunk at the HR Tech Conference in Vegas. Their definition of "development" means you do unbelievable work, make yourself uncomfortable daily, and ensure your clients in other departments view you as a star.

4. **The Mentor will give you face time with the most important people in the organization.** The bad news (for people who thought development was a Dale Carnegie class) is you're going to work like a dog and fail more often than you're used to. The good news? You're going to get 70–80 percent of the credit for the success you have. The Mentor will give you access to their leadership peers on a regular basis, which is your opportunity to shine and understand what it's like to serve a leadership team. The Mentor's

not going to steal your work or, more importantly, the credit. They want a great HR function and knows having a team full of stars is the way to get there. You do good, you get the glory.

5. **The Mentor will take large amounts of s*** from people who matter in order to give you space to do great work.** You do bad, the Mentor protects you. Their DNA (we'll talk about this next) is wired to play the political game at the highest levels of your company. They are a lobbyist in this capacity, and you'll never know the effort they extend related to the space they are providing you.

6. **The Mentor expects you'll leave in 3–5 years if they can't provide the career path or next step you need, and they'll think something's wrong if you don't.** The Mentor helps their direct reports build unbelievable portfolios of work. They bounced from their last company to take the leadership role they are in now. They'll think something's wrong if you don't do the same. They are looking to build a family tree in the world of HR that would rival Bill Belichick or Gregg Popovich, meaning lots of senior HR leaders get their chance to lead an HR function after working for them.

When Jill was stepping into the conference room at Grocery-Runner in the intro of this chapter, she was getting ready to do work on behalf of the HR function and her direct reports. The Mentor is a master at creating space for people who work for them to be successful. It's an up at dawn, pride-swallowing siege that they will never fully tell you about.

Let's Check the DNA of the Mentor, Shall We?

The behavioral DNA of the Mentor is driven by balance. In order to be a leader capable of maximizing their team motivationally while dealing with the dysfunction and narcissism of the senior team, a mix of traits is needed.

The mentor never gets too high—or too low. There's too much to do, and overreaction is not in their DNA.

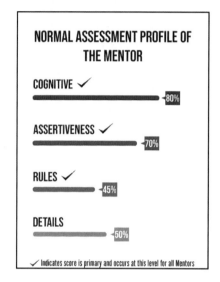

Figure 15.2. Scorecard of the Mentor

Primary DNA Characteristics of The Mentor

» **High Cognitive/High Processing Speed.** There's a lot going on in the world of any senior HR leader, so it makes sense that the Mentor needs high cognitive skills to make quick, accurate decisions.

Updates are the currency of the Mentor. They have updates coming from their direct reports verbally. They have data reports flowing through their laptop on the hour. They are evaluating the hot takes and opinions of how their team is doing by influencers up and down the organization. At times, their ability to deal with all the incoming signals and make the right call is seen as instinctual. But it's not instincts—it's processing speed that rivals the brain of your MacBook Pro combined with the memory of a premium cloud account with Google Drive.

» **Mid to High Assertiveness.** Unlike profiles like the Assassin, it's not uncommon for the Mentor to score something below a 90th percentile assertiveness score. For a senior level HR leader to be classified as a "Mentor," anything above the median assertiveness score is functional, with the 75th to 90th percentile being optimum. HR pros with assertiveness scores in the 90th percentile and above confront everything. They win a lot of battles, but often lose collaboration style points which can come back to haunt them in the long run. Mentors have enough assertiveness to engage as necessary, but often pick their timing for confrontation carefully. This DNA marker, along with high cognitive skills, helps the Mentor win in corporate politics. They see the game, consider all inputs, and engage when the time is right. But their M.O. isn't to win today's argument; it's to maximize their team's ability to do great work on behalf of the organization.

» **Low to Mid Rules Orientation.** In order to be classified as a Mentor, senior-level HR pros can't be high rules. High rules orientation scores indicate a leader will value policy, process and order over all else, which can stifle innovation. The Mentor generally has a low-mid Rules Orientation score that falls somewhere between the 25th and 50th percentile.

One of the great characteristics of the Mentor is their ability to enable experimentation across their team, which is the key to fostering innovation. But unlike profiles to the far right of the 9 Faces of HR, their moderately low Rules Orientation score creates balance. They don't tell their team that there are no rules. To the contrary, they encourage them to experiment while reminding them they'll be held accountable to seek change in a collaborative fashion with peers from other departments.

Their moderately low rules score gives them comfort as everything appears in chaos around them. They are not one to freak out.

Secondary DNA Characteristic of The Mentor

» **Detail Orientation.** As a senior-level HR pro, detail orientation is the least important variable to identifying a Mentor. Since their organizational level generally comes with administrative support, a Mentor can survive without high details orientation, and most Mentors have mid-range details scores. In addition, high detail orientation scores generally push senior-level HR pros to the left of the 9 Faces of HR grid as they become less comfortable in chaotic corporate environments.

If you've ever had a good to great relationship with an HR leader who allowed you to chase interesting work and protected or encouraged you when you failed, odds are you were working for the Mentor. If you haven't worked for the Mentor, you should try to find one next time you change jobs.

Quiz—How to Tell If You'll Be Running HR at a Great Company in the Next Ten Years

I get it. You're an HR manager or director, and you're wondering if you're on track to take the big chair in HR in the next decade. As luck would have it, I'm equipped with a crystal ball and the right amount of confidence and swagger to predict your future. Lucky you!

The world is changing, and the people paying the bills want different things from HR. *Here's a quick quiz involving five things to look inward at and determine if you've got what it takes to lead an HR team* and be a viable partner to the business leaders who will hire you in the next ten years. Remember, I'm talking about leading HR, not being a part of an HR team.

Let's go to the quiz! Answer yes/no related to who you are (no cheating!), keep a tally, and we'll score it together:

1. **You've got a world-class processor upstairs.** This means you're better than most at taking large amounts of information and making quick, accurate decisions. It's okay to take your time in other roles, but as a future HR leader, you'll be expected to be as quick as the strategy consultants with your opinions and proposed solutions.

2. **You're as assertive as the salespeople in your organization.** Great HR people have always needed to be assertive, but the need for comfort with confrontation continues to escalate. Chaos is everywhere, and if you're going to operate efficiently, you're going to need to mix it up on a daily basis. You can be professional and still challenge others who are trying to play you, your department, or your company.

3. **You're comfortable with no rules at all.** HR people have always been good at creating structure, but HR leaders are increasingly being asked to value structure less as we get further into this century. You'll find that as you create your HR team, it's easy to find HR people to help you execute structured solutions. It's harder to find HR people who don't want anything to do with the operations manual and instead want to develop the best solution for the situation at hand. Things change too rapidly these days for the old status quo to stick. High challenge, low rules, and slightly ADHD HR leaders are on the rise.

4. **You are organized enough at the leadership level to execute.** Many of you would guess that low rules in turn means low details. The reality is that detail orientation exists outside of rules orientation, and low rules with mid- to high-level detail orientation is a very hot profile across executives of all types—including HR. Low rules/high details mean you have the ability to dream AND to execute.

5. **You've got skin like a fat, old rhino.** When you receive bad news or the rare glimmer of negative feedback, you're down for about thirty seconds before recovering and moving on. Companies are increasingly looking for HR leaders who aren't afraid to fail. Failure is a necessary byproduct of attempting to add value. Safe isn't going to cut it any longer.

Let's score it! Add up your "yes" responses to whether you really deliver each of these five features, then use this key to score where you are:

> **+5—Welcome to the club.** If you are who you say you are, I'd like your resume for my clients, even if you're twenty-eight- freaking years-old.

> **+4—Yes, please.** You missed on one thing—you're still a player.

> **+3—I'm going to call you an HR "citizen."** Good enough to get what the business line owners are talking about. Missing a DNA strand or two, but more than serviceable. You're probably going to be working for someone younger than you in the next ten years, but that's okay because you'll add value and they'll still depend on you.

> **+2—The world needs ditch-diggers too.** There's still something for you to do in most HR departments with any size, but it's not leading the function. You're good enough, you're smart enough, and gosh darn it, people like you. But you're going to cap out at the manager level.

> **+1—Darwin called.** He said the kids these days are growing the HR equivalent of opposable thumbs, and I don't see any thumb buds on the sides of your hand stumps. Too bad.

That's my list of the behavioral traits I see in play as we move towards the next decade. Will there still be HR leaders who scored a +1 or +2 on this list? Yes.

Will the replacements for those leaders look like their predecessors? My intel says no way.

16

The Judge

Know Your Role and Shut Your Mouth

"I really don't have a clue about what you're
trying to accomplish with this project."

The conference room table got quiet when Andrea showed her frustration. It always got quiet when this happened. Her direct reports had a name for it: *collaboration interruptus.*

Andrea was the senior vice president of HR at McDonald Inc. She always said the line of business didn't matter because they were involved in so many things as a conglomerate, if one venture failed, another one would pick up the slack. McDonald was like a venture capital firm in that way, if venture capital firms had

Figure 16.1. Andrea the Judge

ten thousand employees and supported businesses as wide-ranging as healthcare software to chicken farms.

133

Andrea missed the days when it was mostly chicken farms. Back then, she could encourage the team to dominate the I-9 situation, prepare for ICE raids, and she didn't have to listen to kids proposing wild projects that the technology division of McDonald Inc. supposedly needed.

She looked again at the name of the agenda item that she had just heard a ten-minute pitch on:

> Project Name: Sourcing Database with A.I Functionality
> Proposed Budget: 50K
>
> Division Focus: Technology
>
> Requestor: Becky Davis, Talent Acquisition Project Manager

The kids kept getting younger. With an HR team of seventy-two FTEs, Andrea couldn't really know everyone, and quality time with non-direct reports had increasingly been limited to project updates and proposals for new initiatives and expenditures.

Andrea didn't know much about A.I., or sourcing for that matter. She did know that a lot of things were broken in talent acquisition. She also knew that every sub-department in HR needed tools and money to be successful, but she didn't think much of tools that didn't help HR run the people side of the business with more command and control.

"I think you probably should focus on the stuff that's broken, Becky."

More uncomfortable silence. After five seconds, Becky recovered enough to ask if there was other information she could provide on the tool in question, or how it would be used. Andrea waved off the need quickly and thanked Becky for coming in.

Becky looked startled and stunned, like a fan of Duke basketball would look right after a school like Northwestern Southern State beat them in the NCAA Tournament. Andrea's director of talent acquisition (and Becky's boss) stood up to walk Becky out.

Of the six direct reports remaining, only one was making eye contact with Andrea. It was Monica, the one who had been telling Andrea she needed to change and start modernizing her HR function. Monica had a look on her face that landed somewhere between "Really?" and "You just confirmed to me that you 100 percent are Darth Vader."

Andrea broke the silence with a remark meant to add levity to the situation.

"You know what was a good project? The time that one guy proposed we do an HR campaign to get employees to stop calling us 'McDonald's.' That was value added!"

Everybody laughed but Monica. Andrea's CEO hated it when employees called the company "McDonald's," for obvious reasons. The 100K PR campaign had been greenlit in record time. The CEO loved it, and Andrea loved it when the CEO was happy with HR.

The Judge Didn't Get Here by Endorsing Failure

Within the 9 Faces of HR profile, the Judge is a senior-level HR pro with low ability/willingness to innovate, drive change, or add incremental value. The profile of Andrea provides a quality snapshot into the mind of the Judge.

The Judge has a simple mandate: enforce rules and limit risk.

The Judge didn't make it to the top by greenlighting a bunch of innovative stuff and watching half of it fail. They got to the top the old-fashioned way—by respecting the command and control roots of HR, delivering to the manageable expectations of their peers, and being an absolute master of the political game inside their company.

Evolved Command and Control Marks
the DNA of The Judge

Know your role and shut your mouth. The Judge is a talented HR leader, but they view "vision" as something that's best left to marketing. They are here to manage the ground game of HR, ensuring base services are delivered, lawsuits are minimized (and won when they happen), and that the team doesn't threaten the authority of the leaders and managers of the client group they serve.

Let's take a look at the behavioral DNA that makes this leader tick.

Primary DNA Characteristics of the Judge

» **High Rules Orientation.** Like the profiles below them within the 9 Faces of HR model (Machine and Cop), the Judge's worldview is shaped first and foremost by a high Rules Orientation. Structure provides predictability in the Judge's eyes, which means no one gets surprised, everyone knows what's expected, and criticism is low as long as services are delivered. As an HR leader, being high rules also drives their view of attempts at innovation by their HR team. Projects involving new ways of doing things lead to decreased predictability, which drives the Judge nuts. As a result, the Judge isn't an incubator for professional growth for younger team members in the same way other senior profiles are (The Mentor, The Natural).

» **High Assertiveness.** Unlike the profiles below them within the 9 Faces of HR model (Machine, Cop), the Judge always has an Assertiveness score that lands in the top quartile, with many Judges landing in the top 10 percent. This DNA marker makes the Judge exceptional at enforcing the HR platform they have created. They won't blink when the need to confront anyone (their team, vendors, client group leaders). In addition to willingness to confront, the high assertiveness score also makes the

Judge a political master as a member of the company's leadership team. They are fearless when the need to use political leverage arises, often reminding their peers subtly that they can't support their failures unless they support them fully. The use of this tactic is another reason they manage risk aggressively—failure in their department lowers their ability to leverage the failures of others.

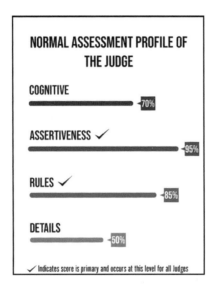

Figure 16.2. Scorecard for the Judge

Secondary DNA Characteristics of the Judge

» **Variable Cognitive/High Processing Speed.** While more processing speed clearly benefits the Judge, mid-range cognitive abilities are adequate for them to achieve their goals. Rules and assertiveness are the primary markers.

» **Variable Detail Orientation.** It's not uncommon for The Judge to have high detail orientation, but mid-range detail orientation is appropriate as well. The Judge's rise from the ranks is fueled by their high assertiveness, a marker different from the profiles below them within the 9 Faces of HR model (Machine, Cop).

A smart Judge with low to mid-range details orientation will be surrounded with high detail people, which is what you would expect any self-aware megalomaniac to do.

The Judge made it. They are going to make sure they stay on top.

Things on the Judge's "To-Do" List

Everyone reading this book knows a Judge in their lives. Some love the Judge, some hate the Judge, but for the most part, everyone respects the Judge. They climbed the ladder, arrived, and are now running the show.

How Judges run the show is pretty consistent across industries and geography, with laser focus occurring in the following areas:

- » **Limit dumpster fires.** The Judge likes rules, which in turn means they hate surprises. They learned a long time ago that a great way to prevent surprises is to not create self-inflicted wounds, which is a fancy way of saying "don't take risks." As a result, your Judge generally reacts negatively to anything with a risk of failing greater than five percent.
- » **Focus on compliance and risk management as the core service of HR.** Limiting risk and feeding their high rules DNA means the Judge is uniquely focused on areas like compliance, which makes them a great fit for some sectors, and misplaced in others. Odds are the Judge grew up in an industry where hard HR compliance is necessary for the business to thrive.
- » **Stay in the position they are in**—by any means necessary. The Judge finally arrived in the leadership role. They are talented politically and not really thinking about "the next thing." What's next you ask? They are focused on cashing in on the next fifteen years, right where they are at. See items one and two for the roadmap on how they plan to do that.

Never mistake low innovation with low talent when it comes to the Judge. They are plenty talented. Their focus isn't on new things; it's on brutal execution.

HR Jobs the Judge Is a Great Fit For

Is the Judge the right fit for your company? That probably depends on the industry you're in. Here's a list of the industries the Judge can thrive in:

» **Manufacturing.** Anytime fingers can leave the possession of a worker based on a simple mistake, risk management makes sense.
» **Financial Services.** The conservative nature of this industry calls for an HR leader who operates with an eye toward security, trust, and execution. The Judge has all of that and more.
» **Healthcare.** So many things can go wrong with patient care, right? The Judge is often a safe choice in this sector.

Note that not every HR leader in these industries is a Judge. Many stars in these industries fit the Mentor profile as well. If you're talking a leader in one of the above industries, ask them questions about where the best candidates for their HR team come from. If they've made multiple hires from outside their industry, odds are you're looking at a Mentor, not a Judge.

As good as those industries feel to the Judge, there are other sectors where the Judge *can't* be successful, including the following:

» **Software and Tech.** The Judge was found working in the Bay Area. They laughed at the need to build a "big a** slide" in the middle of the office space. Turns out, that's exactly what was needed. #chaos
» **Consulting.** Hire the smartest young people you can find, work them to death, and include and empower them in the ideation

related to building a great company. The Judge was with you on the hiring youngsters and working them to death part. You completely lost them in the whole "collaboration" thing.

» **Any other company or industry where intellectual capital is the product.** Simply put, any company with intellectual capital as the core product means more employee involvement, more focus on engagement, learning, and development, and a whole lot more areas that end with "-ment." Judges hate added focus on the suffix "-ment."

» **Working for a visionary leader that wants to build culture.** The Judge likes the iron glove that compliance can provide. Building culture usually means fewer rules and less structure. Plus, they secretly hate leaders who talk about culture constantly.

Why the Judge Chases Away Certain Types of Talent

Earlier in this chapter, you got a taste of Andrea's (a Judge) reaction to an employee's proposal to dip into the A.I. scene via a recruiting sourcing tool.

Andrea nixed that idea and did not use bumpers in the feedback that was provided. The Judge doesn't put a high value on innovation or chasing ideas that might lead to innovation. It's simply how they're wired. Their assertiveness means that reality can be communicated in a way that some would call "harsh."

One outcome of this worldview is that lower level team members on the opposite side of the 9 Faces of HR model (Rookie, Assassin) don't feel valued or see growth opportunities in HR organizations led by the Judge.

Both the Rookie and the Assassin are high innovation/high change. They're going to have ideas, they're going to want to work on things that enhance their career, and they desire a general sense of being developed for "what's next."

The risk management sensibilities of the Judge often shut down ideas and deprioritizes development across the HR function.

Over time, profiles like the Rookie and the Assassin will leave HR organizations led by the Judge. Career-minded to a fault, these up-and-comers will leave once they figure out that the worldview of the Judge will limit their growth.

This type of turnover doesn't faze the Judge. Development efforts that are real are often messy, and the Judge doesn't budget for risk or failure.

Lessons from Uber: Sometimes Your HR Job Changes

If there's one thing that's true in HR, it's that the HR leader who is right for a company today may not be right for the same company five years from now. Things change. Companies grow. New leaders come in; new strategies are developed and deployed.

If you're really lucky as a founder, your company experiences exponential growth that causes you to need a different type of HR leader. Hopefully your current HR leader can grow to meet the need, but change is often needed.

The company Uber fits that example, and in 2016 they had a trade out—an early CHRO named Renee Atwood left, and a new, dramatically different one, entered. Here's the rundown of the change in 2016 from *Business Insider* to set up our analysis:

> Uber is bringing in Liane Hornsey, a longtime VP at Google and current operating partner at SoftBank, to be its new chief HR officer.
>
> The move gives Uber a seasoned executive with public company experience to help manage the $66 billion ride-hailing service's rapidly swelling ranks and to guide it through the various challenges facing startups as they evolve into giant businesses.
>
> Travis Kalanick announced the hiring in an email to Uber employees on Friday, calling her "one of the most sought-after 'people people' in the world," according to a source inside the ride-hailing company.

The opening at Uber, one of the fastest-growing companies in tech, became available in July when its former head of HR Renee Atwood left to join Twitter. Atwood had been at the company from when it was 605 employees to more than 5,000.

Hornsey's LinkedIn profile shows she had spent nine years at Google as its vice president of global people operations before she moved to the sales side as a VP, reporting to Nikesh Arora.

She followed Arora to SoftBank International in September 2015 to be its chief administrative officer and operating partner, helping other startups with their HR needs. Arora left his position in June 2016, and now Hornsey's departure follows nearly six months after. Hornsey will start at Uber in January.

Some things come to mind here from an HR leadership perspective:

» **If you look at the LinkedIn profile of Renee Atwood (former CHRO at Uber, then at Twitter, and at this writing the CPO at Nubank in Brazil), you'll see a pretty good background.** Now go look at the background of Liane Hornsey. Neither one is right or wrong—they are just different. One is about growth and the other one is more mature from a career perspective, focused on things that a company of over five thousand people focuses on.

» **Atwood joined Uber when it had 605 employees and left at the time it had grown to 5,000** (Both FTE numbers do not count driving contractors). Anyone in HR would tell you that those are two dramatically different companies as evidenced by the size, and the fact that it's Uber only adds an exponential factor to that difference.

» **Uber was a unicorn and increased market cap from $13B to $70B during Atwood's tenure.** Atwood chose to leave for a cool company in Twitter, albeit one that doesn't have a clear path moving forward.

» **Uber also had a clear cultural change mandate when the HR leadership change was made.** Simply put, the hard-charging, take no prisoners leadership of Kalanick had created a toxic culture. That culture impacted employees in a negative way (reported alleged broad-based harassment, bullying) and the need to change that culture drove the HR leadership change.

I think Atwood's background was very strong. She was a former client group leader at Citi and Google, got a great opportunity at Uber, and was around for the boom—I really like that progression.

Uber's issues at the time of the change (2016) were dramatically different today than they were in 2014. The fact they changed out the CHRO—a seemingly voluntary move by Atwood before Hornsey was brought in—is evidence pointing to the fact that the HR pro you have today may not be right for you tomorrow.

If you're a CEO out there, looking at your HR leader (and determining whether you still have a fit as you grow) should be as important as looking at your CFO's fit for the stage your company is in.

A Cautionary Tale for HR Pros at All Levels

Whether you're an early-, mid-, or senior-level HR pro, at some point in the future you're going to get a new boss (see later chapter for more extensive notes on this). When that happens, you're interviewing all over again. As much as that may seem unfair, it's fundamentally true.

Understanding which of the 9 Faces you are is key. Having the self-awareness that comes with knowing which face you are is a huge advantage because you can understand how you transmit clues about what's most important to you as an HR pro and seek to maximize or minimize those signals based on who you are talking to.

Dig deeper into the Uber scene and it's clear that Atwood helped the company scale recruiting, moving from 605 to 5,000 employees in the time she was there. As the evidence mounted that the culture was out of control (note: I'm not sure Atwood could have done anything to prevent that), she either got or it was or mutually agreed a change was needed.

Postmortem: Changing HR Leaders Doesn't Always Work

Of course, I can't use the example of Uber without following up on the Atwood to Hornsey change.

Hornsey was brought in to Uber as a form of mature, adult HR leadership to deal with and turn around the cultural toxicity typically referred to as a "bro" culture. If I use my 9 Faces of HR model, the move suggested Uber was attempting to move to left of the grid—more command, control, and traditional HR to deal with the 2016 circumstances.

The seasoned executive (Hornsey) joined the company a month before former engineer Susan Fowler penned an infamous blog post talking about the rampant sexual harassment and sexism she endured at Uber. As head of the HR department, Hornsey served as one of the company's top spokespersons on issues regarding diversity and discrimination throughout the upheaval that followed.

She was gone by mid-2018. At an all-hands meeting at headquarters in 2017 to share the results of a four-month investigation by former Attorney General Eric Holder into Uber's workplace culture, Hornsey led an awkward moment by asking everyone in the room "to stand up and give each other a hug," as reported by New York Times reporter Mike Isaac.

You read that right. She ordered hugs while harassment investigations were being reviewed by Obama's former Attorney General.

Hornsey resigned in mid-2018 in the midst of a third-party firm investigating allegations that she routinely dismissed internal racial discrimination complaints.

Uber probably thought they needed the Judge when they hired Hornsey to help the company grow up quickly. The pace of change at Uber underscores how important it is to match the right HR leadership with company stage and the most pressing talent issues across your organization.

17

The Assassin

Why join the Navy when you can be a pirate?
—Steve Jobs

Meet Chole, a Trained Assassin

Chloe didn't think much before she pulled the trigger on the email that would start a small civil war in her own department. As a relatively new HR manager for Trifecta Inc., one of the projects she had been handed was the repeat implementation of the new Applicant Tracking System (ATS), which failed last year and had never been launched.

Chloe liked her day-to-day work as an HR manager, but she *loved* the project work that Joan, the SVP of HR, sent her way from time to time. The day-to-day got boring, but the turnaround projects Joan provided never failed to entertain Chloe.

In a sea of details, Chloe understood that the single reason the implementation had failed was that seven recruiters

Figure 17.1. Chloe the Assassin

Trifecta employed refused to play along, and no one really checked them on their unwillingness to change.

Now here was Chloe, a year after the failed implementation at 6:00 am on a Monday, getting ready to send an email to that recruiting team informing them that the side spreadsheets they used to track candidates had been removed from the server, with the data tracked in those sheets uploaded to the ATS and the sheets being deleted both locally and in the cloud once that data transfer had been verified.

Chloe thought about titling the email, "Burn the Ships," a shout out to her useless history major and the famous quote from Hernan Cortes when he arrived in the new world and refused to allow his men the comfort of a Plan B should they fail. She thought the better of that and typed, "ATS Data Transfer," then wondered if she should send a quick note to Rick, the lead of the recruiting group, to prepare him for the blowback before she sent the broader note to the team.

"F**k it," Chloe thought as she pressed the send button on that email with a CC to Rick. Let the confrontations begin.

What Is an Assassin?

The Assassin is one of the most distinctive personas in the 9 Faces of HR. Fast thinking, ready for change and not really giving two s***s about other people's feelings, the Assassin is the person you call or assign when you know people are going to resist change that needs to happen, but you don't have the stomach to deal with it.

The Assassin is defined as a mid-career HR pro with the highest ability to innovate, drive change, and add value in the 9 Faces of HR model. The Assassin is a specialist, and their superpower is making change happen. Assassins live among us on HR teams, at times underperforming in the day-to-day tasks of their HR role, but they shine on projects with a lot of moving parts involving multiple influencers.

Things to know about the Assassin:

» They're smart as hell.
» They like chaos.
» People respect them.
» People grow to hate them.
» They do difficult things that others on HR teams can't or won't do.
» They sleep like babies after doing difficult things.

With notes like that, what could possibly go wrong with the Assassin? Let's dig into what makes them tick.

Let's Check the DNA of the Assassin, Shall We?

The behavioral DNA of the Assassin is clear and distinct, the same way the DNA of a shark can't be mistaken for any other animal. Sharks swim, and Assassins drive change. Film at 11.

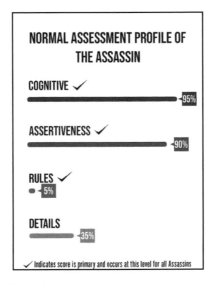

Figure 17.2. Scorecard for the Assassin

Primary DNA Characteristics of The Assassin

» **High Cognitive/High Processing Speed.** The Assassin is well positioned to deal with a lot of data and make quick and accurate decisions. It's almost impossible to overwhelm The Assassin with data, deadlines, and other details that make others frustrated and unable to act. The high processing speed of an Assassin makes them very confident in their decisions, and the decisions often come fast. That speed makes others at times tag the Assassin as "reckless," which is code for, "slow the **** down." But the Assassin won't slow down if asked. If anything, they'll speed up based on their contempt for those around them who aren't willing to *get things done.* Shame on you, normal humans of HR. The Assassin was built for speed.

» **High Assertiveness.** Change doesn't happen without confrontation, and with a top quartile assertiveness score, the Assassin has what they need to drive change. They are generally unafraid to confront people at all levels, and at times it seems like the Assassin is unaware of organizational politics and the merits of "asking" instead of "telling." The Assassin views project lead status as a charter to get things done. They'll view their mission as the most important one in a sea of conflicting organizational priorities, and their high assertiveness helps push their mission to the top. Their assertiveness comes through in face-to-face meetings, email and text communications, and conference calls. They are going to ask for what they need, tell you what to do, and dare you to say no. If you say no, that's just the beginning of the dialogue and process with the Assassin, which is why many people learn to not get in their way.

Hashtags: #me, #myproject, #justdoit, #aggressive

» **Very Low Rules Orientation.** The most important DNA marker in this profile is that the Assassin is bored by static environments. Birds must fly, and Assassins need change in order to feel maximized in any organization. It's important to note the severity of this behavioral marker. To be properly coded as an Assassin, individuals have to score in the bottom 10 percent of the general population related to rules orientation. Low rules orientation means Assassins are never constrained by the way things are currently done. The more rules you have in your organization, the more the Assassin wants to blow it all up and watch it burn. Ever have a member of your team proactively change their office three times in the course of a year? That's a simple environmental marker of a high change/low rules teammate. Whether they are a true Assassin or not depends on the other markers.

Secondary DNA Characteristic of The Assassin

» **Detail orientation.** Assassins trend towards having low to mid scores on detail orientation, primarily because high detail orientation creates a need for order that slows them down. While we've seen Assassins with high detail orientation scores (the other three traits remain very dominant), the general trend is low to mid scores in this area. Variability with this trait causes it to be viewed as secondary to the other markers.

This concludes the lab report on the Assassin. Move over, normal HR people.

The Resume of the Assassin Is Unmistakable and Here's Why

Once the Assassin reaches thirty-two years of age and has a decade of work experience in HR, their resume becomes so distinctive it should be titled, "I like to tear things down for the greater good."

With a resume objective like that, who's buying?

As it turns out, plenty of people. It takes a village to build an HR team capable of accomplishing everything on an HR leader's strategic plan. The skills of the Assassin are always in demand by HR functions looking to modernize and turn a sleepy backwater of transactions into a modern HR machine.

So, you've determined you need an Assassin. How do you spot them on a resume before you have a chance to put them through the behavioral assessment that is part of your process? It's easy if you know what you are looking for: Assassins with a decade or more of experience have a series of two-year stints at the majority of their companies.

It's true. A true young Assassin can't hack it for more than two years at a company early in their career. Here's why:

» **Assassins make a lot of enemies and are often asked to leave.** Assassins piss off an average of 2.4 people per month in your company (I made up that statistic but stay with me) via their actions. Do the math, that's twenty-four people who hate the Assassin per year. By year two, the number creeps towards fifty true enemies, and the negatives start to outweigh the positives. That's problematic. Being asked to leave comes in a lot of different flavors for the Assassin. Sometimes they are fired, but more often than not, they're organized out or are simply assigned to a new line HR position (with a client group of employees and all the needs that come with that) designed to make them hate their lives and leave for another job. Putting an Assassin in charge of payroll will chase them out of your company in under ninety days.

» **Assassins voluntarily leave companies when the pace of change slows, and they get bored.** When you think about transformation in the world of HR, it's safe to say that a new HR leader can get to some form of a steady state within twenty-four months. When that happens, the Assassin is suddenly looking at governing what they have helped to build, and let's just say that Assassins have the same desire to govern as Genghis Kahn did to be the mayor of Kabul. Assassins drive change. They don't manage what they build—at least not for long.

» **Lots of companies say they want change but can't deliver what the Assassin needs once they arrive on the scene.** It's common for Assassins to get sucked in by a recruiting sales pitch on big change, only to arrive at their new company and find the organization has absolutely no appetite for what they're best at. In these occasions, the Assassin doesn't even have access to the tools and data they need to shake things up. They'll try for a year, then put it on autopilot for year two before they bounce to the next big thing.

Need a bonus resume indicator? Look for the person with five 2-year stints, with the description of each stint being focused on the projects they completed rather than a broad description of what their duties were. Assassins tend to outline big wins above all else.

It's a hard knock world for Assassins. They're built for change, and when they deliver the goods, they make enemies. Sometimes they get sold a bill of goods and arrive only to find the most bureaucratic environment possible. They get bored. But they're not stupid—they won't wreck their career by bouncing in six months. They'll put in the time, feed the change addiction some other way (side hustle during working hours), and bounce when appropriate.

The Four Best Ways to Use an Assassin in Your Organization

Everyone reading this knows an Assassin, either as part of your current team or somebody you've worked with in the past. If you're an HR leader reading this, here's a short list of how you can use the Assassin in your organization:

1. **To Drive Big Projects Through the Pipe.** Admit it, you don't have anyone with the edge to do what it takes to get that big system launch complete. Sure, you could give it to

Sally, but she'll give in and you'll end up with a watered-down product. Enter the Assassin.

2. **To Partner with Business Leaders Doing Change with a Big "C."** Let's say you've got a sales force undergoing big changes and a dynamic sales leader who just came in to get it done. You need someone with the moxie to take that on and be respected by the leader, and the Assassin has the DNA to hang in that situation.

3. **Use Them to Be the Agent of Change In an Otherwise Sleepy Department.** You just inherited your HR team, and while they are okay, they're pretty comfortable. Hiring an Assassin is a sure-fire way to make people ponder what's required in the new world order.

4. **Use Them as Your Departmental "Bad Cop."** If you're really self-aware, you may realize you fall to the left of the 9 Faces of HR, or maybe you're just a pleasant person without much stomach for confrontation. That's okay—you do you and hire an Assassin to go kill things when things need killed. Be the good cop you're so comfortable being and outsource the nasty stuff.

Using the Assassin in these ways not only maximizes their utility, but it also maximizes their retention. The Assassin understands you never make a shot that you don't take. Shooters shoot. Haters hate. This is the Assassin's creed.

Bonus

HR Metrics: Stop Measuring You and Start Measuring Them

"How are we looking on time to fill?"
"Why is turnover so high?"

At times, these two questions are the bane of any HR pro's existence. After all, any moderately talented HR pro understands that there are many factors that go into either measurement, just as there are multiple people within the organization who impact the numbers—not just HR.

Still, when requested, most HR pros at multiple levels simply report the numbers and take ownership of each metric.

That just pisses the Assassin off.

If you know anything about the Assassin, you know that their mission is to play offense, not defense. They're smart as hell, uber-aggressive, and don't really care about how it's always been done. With that in mind, The Assassin hears the aforementioned questions and, instead of complying with the request, changes the question. *"Have you ever heard of Hiring Manager Batting Average?"*

Of course, they haven't. The Assassin never asks a question they don't know the answer to. What is the Assassin talking about? Control of the narrative, my friends. The Assassin is changing the question and turning the spotlight away from HR.

Hiring Manager Batting Average Is One
Example of Offense Over Defense

We're digging into the Hiring Manager Batting Average (HMBA) as one example of how you can stop measuring HR and start measuring the business. All HR pros understand that every company has hiring managers who

» Are awful at interviewing and making hiring decisions.
» Can't keep good talent once it is on boarded.

With those realities in mind, a new metric exists called the HMBA. Here's the formula:

Hiring Manager Batting Average:

> All employees hired by a manager over period of time and still with company after one year **divided by** all employees hired by manager over a period of time, including those who have left

Here's a simple example from a hiring manager—eight total hires. Five spent at least a year with the company divided by eight hires overall in time period. The HMBA in this example is .625.

If you like this metric, you know the dirty secret. Hiring Manager Batting Average measures a lot of things that have nothing to do with HR and are instead related to a manager's skill with human capital related issues, including the hiring manager's ability to:

1. make the right selection
2. provide a realistic job preview
3. successfully bring talent onboard
4. engage and stay connected to talent

And at least twenty other non-HR things you can think of, specific to your own organization

That's the HMBA in a nutshell. It's not about HR, it's about the skills of the hiring manager. You could stop there, but to really be effective playing offense instead of defense, you'll have to be a bit more political.

To take it to the next level, you've got to make a choice related to how to report HMBA. You can do it at the company, department, or hiring manager level. It's obvious that the broadest way to report is at the company level, but you're selling yourself short if you stop there. To get real change, you'll need to report HMBA at the departmental or hiring-manager level. Scoreboard time!

Your CEO will see HMBA charts and want to talk about the lowest performing departments. Once the department heads got involved, they'll quickly want to see manager results in their own department to understand who's effective and who's not.

This is exactly what the Assassin wants when they introduce a metric like HMBA that measures others instead of HR. Power. Dialogue. Change.

Metrics Like HMBA Change the Relationship
HR Has with the Business

By introducing a metric like the HMBA, HR isn't focusing on HR, it's focusing on the business. It also underscores the fact that HR can't win unless it's willing to keep score and tell the world who's winning. But the process doesn't stop there—if HR is willing to report on winners and losers in talent-related areas, they have to be quick to offer help to those who aren't winning.

Metrics Like HMBA Help HR Set Up
a Pure Consulting Model

While public reporting on the HMBA won't include the individual manager level, the reporting you do in private must include, and focus on, the individual manager level. By doing this, you're looking to share the data with the functional area and departmental leaders, prove you understand the business, and gain their trust to help them fix the problems.

This is consulting 101—being data-driven and then providing recommendations to help in areas of need.

The Benefits of Playing Offense with
Metrics Outweigh the Risks

The Assassin wouldn't hesitate to use the Hiring Manager Batting Average (HMBA) to change the focus on how HR issues are measured in the organization. Offense is better than defense. Metrics like the HMBA will help you get the attention of the organization, and, as a result, help bring you into consultative conversations with the leaders of your company/divisions/departments.

Of course, metrics that point to issues elsewhere still beg the question—what's your solution for the issues identified? Metrics like the HMBA create more project work almost all of the time.

The Assassin? They are 100 percent down with that.

18

The Fixer

I took care of the autopsy; it's handled.
—Olivia Pope (Kerry Washington) in *Scandal*

Meet Jim, the Fixer

"You're damned if you do, and you're damned if you don't."

Jim thought about what he needed to do before the end of this Tuesday, the one that was going to hell quickly. Sheila from finance had just left his office after unloading to him for seventy-five minutes.

It was an important visit, but Jim wondered if Sheila thought he was her therapist or her HR man-  ager. The last forty-five minutes sure felt like therapy for her, but for him? He was exhausted.

Life at Motorcom wasn't bad for Jim. He was in his seventh year with the company, and he was promoted into the HR manager role two years ago after starting out as an HR coordinator. People always said he was a good guy, and they also commented that he must be a great dad after seeing the photos of his family on his desk.

Figure 18.1. Jim the Fixer

Motorcom was your typical tier three manufacturing partner for a colossal auto plant in the new south. Margins were thin, and the working environment was aggressive. The workforce (1,500 FTEs) was non-union and mostly blue collar. F-bombs and offsite after-work beers were the norm, not the exception.

That informality was a petri dish for employee relations issue. No one knew that better than Jim.

Sheila was an accountant at Motorcom. She had joined the company two years ago and was known as a good performer. Two months ago, she had applied internally for an open accounts payable manager role at the company. Jim was aware that Rick, the director of accounting and finance, had interviewed her for the role.

Apparently, that wasn't all Rick had done with Sheila.

Sheila had dropped by Jim's office today to formally submit a sexual harassment claim. Sheila's story was basic and cut to the chase. Rick had shown a flirting interest in Sheila starting six months ago, and across multiple after-work beer sessions, the interest had grown into a romantic relationship. They'd been sleeping together for four months. Sheila's boss worked directly for Rick. They had kept the relationship secret.

Jim wasn't aware of any rumors, so that checked out on the surface.

When Sheila expressed interest in the AP manager role, Rick told her she should definitely apply. She did, and they spent the formal interview time just shooting the s*** according to Sheila. They had agreed that a formal interview would feel a little forced.

Rick was making the rounds notifying candidates after his selected external candidate (not Sheila) had accepted the AP manager role. He had sent an email to Sheila that followed the same format he sent to everyone else.

To say Sheila was pissed was an understatement. She waited two hours and then came to see Jim in HR. She was adamant that her situation was something called "quid pro quo" harassment. Jim was fairly certain that if he checked her browsing history on the network, he'd see Google searches that morning on "sexual harassment," followed by clicks on "hostile environment," and "quid pro quo."

"This is the job," Jim thought as he tried, and failed, to slouch in his ergonomic office chair after Sheila left.

They always laid the big bags of flaming dog doo on his doorstep to sort through. He wondered if they would come to him as much if he didn't have a reputation for being such a great listener.

Jim started to text his boss, the VP of HR. She was going to love this one.

Great HR Pros with Client Groups Are Always Fixers

Jim is the Fixer in the 9 Faces of HR model, a mid-career HR professional with mid-range ability to innovate, drive change, and add incremental value.

The definition of a fixer in pop culture/business/the mafia goes something like this:

1. A person who makes arrangements for people and helps them out of tight spots.
2. A local hired by a foreign journalist, often as a translator and guide, and often helps the journalist gain access to interviewees and stories.
3. A person or thing that fixes; repairs.

It's notable that the term "fixer" doesn't always comes with the positive connotation depicted by Hollywood. It's often related to organized crime or shady dealings. I'm going to defend the idea of a fixer being tied to HR because lawyers and other professions will sometimes intercede on behalf of clients. When they get involved as fixers, they execute offers of non-nondisclosure agreements in exchange for some benefit or advising people of the potential legal consequences of unduly incriminating others.

Another name for the "fixer" is the "cleaner." Let's look at examples of great "fixer/cleaners" from Hollywood:

» **Harvey Keitel as Winston "The Wolf" Wolfe in *Pulp Fiction*.** Travolta and Samuel L. Jackson had a body. The boss said he was sending "The Wolf" to assist. This news immediately calmed Samuel L. Jackson down, which is hard to do.

» **Kerry Washington as Olivia Pope in *Scandal*.** Professional specializing in "fixing" political situations and scandals. Her character has become a widely watched fashion and style trendsetter, because let's face it, fixers are cool.

» **Jonathan Banks as Mike Ehrmantraut in *Breaking Bad*.** Bald guy engaged by Walter White to do a variety of tasks related to his unique expertise. Not a fashion aficionado, but a great fixer.

» **Patricia Clarkson as Jane Davis in Netflix's *House of Cards***—She can hang out in the white house without an official title and make calls to the Middle East to stand down warring factions if you ask her to. Seems like someone who is good to have around.

» **Liev Schreiber in the title role in Showtime's *Ray Donovan*.** My favorite of the list. He's an NYC transplant running around L.A. cleaning up messes for stars, athletes, and politicians.

If you've watched any of the movies or series these characters starred in, you've got a feel for what a Fixer does. While the Fixer in HR doesn't deal with dead bodies, it's safe to say they deal with a lot of situations on a daily basis that causes them to be flexible.

An employee comes in with their hair on fire about an atrocity that just happened on the second floor. A manager calls with a situation that, if left unchecked, could blow up important work being done that's key to the company's survival. You live your life in HR, which means you could give me one hundred examples of these things in the next ten minutes. Who do those calls come to when

advice or counsel is needed? The mid-level HR manager/director/
HRBP with great judgment and a calm nature.

Those calls come to the Fixer in HR.

Let's Check the DNA of the Fixer, Shall We?

The Fixer has a DNA profile that's decidedly unspectacular, but well
suited for their role. Since Fixers are mid-career HR pros at the manager, director, and HRBP levels with employee client groups, the
preferred DNA profile is one of balance.

What does balance mean when it comes to a professional's
behavioral DNA profile? Think about it this way: extreme scores at
the low or high end of the spectrum for any behavioral characteristic
are usually seen as purely strength or weakness. The reality is that
extreme scores—even when viewed as a significant strength—often
come with a cautionary tale related to how perceived strength can
go wrong in the workplace.

Need an example? Low Sensitivity is seen as a strength by many
because a professional with that trait recovers quickly from harsh
feedback or rejection. That's a good thing. But the same individual
has a hard time with empathy for others and also will struggle with
their sense of urgency at times. Extreme scores are rarely 100 percent good or bad— they are simply best viewed in context for the
situation or job a person finds themselves in.

Fixers are known for their lack of extreme behavioral scores. As
a result, the Fixer profile in the 9 Faces of HR model is the among
the most variable of all the faces. Being in the middle of multiple
behavioral measures is common traits of the Fixer.

HR pros with a flock of employees who rely on them in a client
group must be many things to many people. Balanced behavioral
profiles help them flex and find the right approach based on the
situation at hand.

Employees at all levels trust the balance they feel in the Fixer.

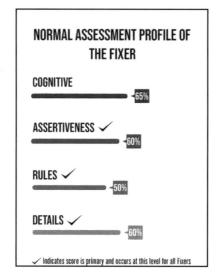

Figure 18.2. Scorecard for Fixer

Primary DNA Characteristics of The Fixer

» **Mid-Range Assertiveness.** While any mid-career HR pro needs enough assertiveness to confront situations and people who need to be confronted, being between the 40th and 70th percentile in assertiveness can make the Fixer appear non-threatening, which is an advantage when getting all the information you can is the priority. The Fixer understands that the slow-and-steady approach often wins and that being too assertive can reduce options to fix whatever problem is in front of them.

» **Mid-Range Rules Orientation.** Being mid-range in rules orientation creates balance, which leads to great counsel about when the time is right to break rules and when the pragmatic approach points the client to the rule book. Great HR pros with client groups understand the right answer is generally preceded by "it depends." The balance of the Fixer in this area means they find the right answer for the client more often than most.

» **Mid-Range Detail Orientation.** Demanding absolute attention to detail means you might be too slow. Ignoring details means you might make unforced errors that are avoidable. The Fixer's mid-range detail orientation score allows them to flex to a level of detail that makes sense for the situation in front of them.

Secondary DNA Characteristics of The Fixer

» **Mid- to High Cognitive/High Processing Speed.** While having more cognitive horsepower is always welcome, having mid-range cognitive speed is not a bad thing for the Fixer. Mid-career jobs in HR serving client groups often come with the need to listen, and mid-range cognitive skills translate nicely into the appearance of patience.

Most of What the Fixer Does Doesn't Show Up on a Report

Being the Fixer in HR doesn't involve a lot of glory. Most of the wins the Fixer tallies in HR can't or won't be covered in reports or discussions of the value HR adds. Let's list some common s***-shows the Fixer handles through conversations, street smarts, and the right action at the right time:

» **An insurance company is playing hardball with cost sharing for an employee's kid who has cancer.** The Fixer makes four calls, semi-threatens someone in the right way, and presto! The kid has their medication paid for.

» **An employee is having difficulty finding their way with a hard charging manager.** The Fixer listens to the employee vent, provides two things the employee could do to make the situation better, and makes the employee promise to try them and report back. The Fixer then turns around and whispers in the manager's ear to give the employee a chance. Things get better and return back to neutral.

» **An underperforming employee is fired and yells they are suing the company as they walk out the door.** The Fixer handles the search for the replacement, and when it's time to make a hire, they have a heart-to-heart talk with the hiring manager on managing risk. They hire the top candidate, who just happens to be the same Title VII protected class as the fired employee. The EEOC charge comes, and the replacement hire makes everyone less interested in the charge, including the judge. Summary judgment is the result. The Fixer smiles when the company's legal counsel calls with the outcome.

» **A talented, but troubled, employee gets stopped on a Saturday night and drug possession charges are filed.** The Fixer gets a call from co-workers in the same department. The Fixer leaves their son's birthday party early on Sunday to talk to the employee in question and convinces them to announce intent for rehab on Sunday night in order to provide leverage against the department's VP's intent to fire them on Monday. An email announcing intent is sent on Sunday, a letter of authorization (LOA) is filed on Monday, and the employee is not fired. The employee does rehab, is still at the company two years later, and has even received a small promotion.

In a way, we're all Fixers in the world of HR. But the middle box in the 9 Faces of HR are where the true Fixers can be found.

The Fixer takes incoming calls from employees. They take walk-ins from managers. They balance the interests of both with calmness and grace that inspires trust.

They make everything better and when necessary, they make the bad stuff go away.

Long live the Fixer in the world of HR.

Bonus
The Five Biggest Lies In HR

The Fixer knows the truth. HR is incredibly hard. So hard that they realize that in an effort to do good work and take care of employees, we've created our own prison. As a result, we're trapped. We've spawned narratives that make the HR function appear like a cross between Mother Teresa and Stuart Smalley, while the team members we serve need more tough love, like a cross between David Chappelle and Ellen Ripley from *Alien*.

As the Fixer does their best to serve their client group, they are confronted with the following whoppers:

> **Lie #1: We're responsible for the work/life balance of team members.** I believe it was a man named Jack Welch who pissed off a bunch of HR pros at the 2009 SHRM Annual Conference in New Orleans by riffing that "there's no such thing as work/life balance, there are work/life choices." I've never met a star who didn't absolutely out-work the competition for promotions, yet our HR universe still talks endlessly about the search for balance. If you're a regular team member reading this, the reality is that the business world is chaotic, and everyone's kind of winging it to a certain extent. Most companies try to keep staffing levels relative to the work at hand (more revenue always helps in that regard!), but it's always going to feel like a free-for-all at times.
>
> **The Truth:** You're responsible for your own work/life balance, and if you want more money, promotions, and fame,

you're going to have to work harder than those around you. As Neutron Jack says, it's your choice.

Lie #2: It's the company's desire to provide strong benefits to all team members. How many shades of gray are there on the color wheel? While we like to take care of team members, if it wasn't part of the American healthcare system and a competitive necessity related to talent, we'd be out of the benefits business so fast it would make Usain Bolt seem slow. Of course, the biggest component to this lie is our unwillingness to hold you accountable for your own health. We'll talk about our cost increases during open enrollment, but most HR functions never really try to change behavior through incentives or penalties.

The Truth: We're not your mom. We only provide benefits because it's an expectation and we have to in order to compete in the talent game. You'll have to take the cost increases we give you as a result, and if we ever get brave enough to try to change the behavior of the outliers, we'll find we're too late due to a legislative environment that protects those making unhealthy choices.

Lie #3: We're into pay for performance. Everyone loves seeing a high performer get a 10 percent raise just for being a star, unrelated to a promotion. It doesn't happen enough, and the reason is pretty simple. In this Darwinian world we call global business, cost pressure is everywhere. As a result, we've got to budget for salary increases, and then live by the budget to make sure razor-thin margins stay intact. That means that in order to give Sally the superstar an eight percent increase at review time, we've got to give nothing to Johnny and Rickey, who are good cogs in the wheel but average at best.

The Truth: We (business leaders and HR pros) need average performers to make the business formula work. In a world where 90 percent of team members think they're in the top 10 percent of all performers, we're screwed from the jump.

Lie #4: We only want "A" players. I gave Neutron Jack some love earlier about work/life balance, so allow me now to take a Tonya Harding-like whack at his kneecaps. Like many of you, I used to love GE's sexy idea of thought leadership promoting the notion you're either up or out, and that our companies should be on a quest to fill our entire ranks with "A" players.

The Truth: Having all A players doesn't work. We can't find enough of you, and even if we could, the world needs ditch diggers too. We need steady people who come into the office, crank out a solid day's work, don't bitch, and don't act like divas when the company doesn't stop operations to thank them personally.

Lie #5: Everyone's equal here. It's true that as HR pros we are the stewards of ensuring discrimination doesn't occur in the organizations we serve. While the world's still not a perfect place, the American workplace has progressed eons in relation to people of different backgrounds having equal opportunity to succeed. However, it gets dicey once individual performance becomes visible. At that point, no one is truly equal because of different contribution levels to the enterprise.

The Truth: Everyone's equal until we see business results, then decisions get made, and conflicts are resolved with an eye towards production. The good news is that producing results is free of bias towards race, gender, or national origin. The bad news is that it feels unfair that someone with a drinking problem gets three strikes instead of two because they were the top performing salesperson nationally. Welcome to the show kid, where the curveballs curve and all the hotels have room service.

Employees are addicted to these lies. While HR has always had a role in advancing these whoppers, the Fixers of HR didn't start the fire. They're simply doing the best they can in hourly interactions with employees, and they're attempting to keep the company between the ditches. God bless the Fixers of HR.

19

The Cop

He sees the uniform and he runs? He did it.
—Detective Vic Mackey (Michael Chiklis) in *The Shield*

Respect the Badge, Fool

"Have you documented that?"

It was a fair question. Alesha knew the answer before she asked. Randy never documented anything or thought to get HR involved when things went sideways with an employee, but he was always indignant when he couldn't fire someone on his terms.

Randy was the classic sales leader. He brought home the bacon and thought that meant he could do whatever he wanted to do. In some ways he was right, and that always made Alesha mad—successful salespeople doing whatever they wanted while the rest of company had to play by the rules.

Randy had made the mistake of sharing in the leadership team meeting that Lawrence, an account executive who had been with BitDome

Figure 19.1. Alesha the Cop

(a telecom making a pivot to becoming a cloud provider) for six months, was struggling.

Information was power, and Alesha liked the power that rules provided.

"You know there's a progressive discipline policy and a performance improvement plan (PIP) for sales at BitDome, right Randy?" she asked.

Of course, he knew. Still, Alesha loved taking charge and addressing managerial renegades in public. Alesha could feel the smile coming from the back of her head. She pushed her tongue against the back of her teeth as hard as she could to prevent the grin from breaking through.

As a director of HR at the mid-size company with a vacant VP of HR job in the process of being filled, Alesha had been asked to participate in the weekly leadership team meetings as the representative from HR. She had attended the sessions for the last two months, and she was gradually becoming more of a participant than an observer.

Randy had screwed up. Alesha had served sales as part of her client group for the last two years, and she knew his sloppy consistency and execution better than anyone. He looked angry for a split second, then calm as he turned to the CEO and answered Alesha.

"No question the process and policies are important. I'm just not sure if we can afford to keep a non-performing rep on board with the revenue challenges we have. Of course, that might depend on how deep the sales recruiting pipeline is. Any thoughts on how that looks, Alesha?"

The 180 degree turn to focusing on the current state of recruiting hit Alesha like a sucker punch. Alesha had many talents but running recruiting as an unnamed interim VP of HR wasn't one of them. There wasn't a sales recruiting pipeline, or any pipeline, for that matter.

The sudden change of topic shook Alesha so much she didn't even put together the obvious point—if there wasn't a candidate to quickly plug in, that meant Randy could take his time and work through the PIP steps with Lawrence.

A couple of awkward seconds passed. Phil, the CEO, broke the silence by exhaling loudly, throwing his hands together and asking Alesha to work with Randy, give him what he needs, and then work Lawrence out in the next two to three weeks. A couple of VPs appeared sympathetic to Alesha based on their facial expressions.

Carol, the VP of marketing, approached Alesha in the hallway after the meeting.

"When it comes to revenue vs. rules—revenue wins every time. Keep your head up."

Alesha wasn't sure what had just happened. She was right, rules are rules. But she had lost the match with Randy, and it wasn't even close.

Alesha retracted her official application for the VP of HR job the next morning. Two days passed, and she still hadn't heard anything from the CEO.

I'm the Company Cop, and I'm Here to Help

The Cop is an HR persona that everyone knows. HR used to be called personnel, which served as a shout-out to its administrative roots. We've been preventing bad stuff from happening ever since.

In the 9 Faces of HR, the Cop is a mid-career HR pro (HR manager or HR director depending on the size of company) with low ability to innovate, drive change, or add incremental value. They thrive on structure and saying "no" as a means of maintaining control and minimizing risk.

Let's Check the DNA of the Cop, Shall We?

Everything about the Cop is designed to command and control the focus of your HR function. It's not a good or bad thing, it's just how they are wired.

As the HR pro with a low ability and willingness to innovate, drive change, and add incremental value moves from early career to mid-career in your company, the stakes naturally get higher. Your company needs to understand what it wants out of an HR manager and HR pro with this common profile in order to ensure the work that's going to be asked of them is a fit for their motivation and world view.

Let's get people paid on time! Let's get that employee handbook done! We're going to need some polices for the handbook—what's our stance on dating other employees? Maybe they could both sign a form waiving the liability in that situation?

The Cop doesn't do chaos. They are the "organizational safety" designed to limit risk and advance the ball three yards at a time. The profile below will illustrate why:

Primary DNA Characteristics of The Cop

» **High Rules Orientation.** The Cop has a high rules orientation score, which means they long to manage the HR function and the company by policy and established procedure with limited exceptions. Exceptions feel like a disease to the Cop. High Rules as a behavioral marker is one of the reasons the Cop can be at risk when new leaders come into the company. New leaders have different experiences with HR at past companies, and they right-fully look to HR for innovation on the people practices side. The DNA of the Cop prevents them from naturally contributing to this need in times of change.

» **High Detail Orientation.** The Cop is organized and values completing tasks above all else as a part of their high detail orientation score. People who don't manage details as well as they do drive them crazy. As a result, the Cop is great at getting things done. When left to their own devices, the Cop will choose to work on task-oriented items rather than attempting to develop ideas from scratch. In times of change or when the organization has an increased need for innovation from HR, this natural inclination to complete tasks can put the Cop at risk.

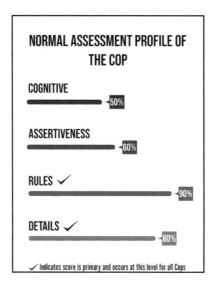

Figure 19.2. Scorecard for the Cop

Secondary DNA Characteristics of Cop

» **Assertiveness.** Cops can display a wide range of assertiveness scores but always have the aforementioned high rules/high details profiles. Cops with low assertiveness scores simply rely on policy and procedure structure, reminding people to comply. Cops with high assertiveness scores are more likely to aggressively engage renegades (like Alesha in the intro). See the final section in this chapter for creative ways that Cops says no as their relative assertiveness scores rise.

» **Cognitive/High Processing Speed.** More processing speed is always welcomed but is not a requirement for the Cop. Embedded in their DNA and the world in which they are most comfortable, the knowledge the Cop needs is finite and established by policy and procedure included in institutional documents like the employee handbook.

High Rules and High Details. There's only one function that's a better fit for that profile than traditional command and control HR—accounting. It's safe to say that college kids who love command and control environments but aren't especially good with numbers could find a great home in traditional HR.

The 5 Ways HR Cops Say "No" at Your Company

Some of you are saying, that's it? Cops say "no" and that defines their lives?

Correct. (I can't say "yes" in a section that's 100 percent about saying no). Turns out, the Cop says no in some comprehensive and creative ways inside your company and HR function. Here are five unique ways cops say "no" at your company.

1. **No, you can't do that because it's in violation of our policy.** The easiest part of the no playbook for the Cop. There's a policy against that, and if you go against the corporate policy, attacking traditional command and control HR function. The Cop doesn't care that the policy sucks. Maybe you suck. If fact, if you don't play by the rules, the Cop is pretty sure that you're an awful person. Rules are rules, no exceptions, sister. "There's a policy against you programming Ginger's phone to forward you all of her emails."

2. **No, you can't do that because you'll get fired as a result.** Also, simple, but a little more serious since it involves a direct

threat to fire someone. Violating policy and getting written up is one thing, but when the Cop tells someone the company will skip all steps of corrective action (something the Cop loves dearly) and fire them, they are making a statement. Threats to harm are a key part of the Cop's playbook of saying no. It's just easier than listening to all the reasons they should say yes.

3. **No, you can't do that because I don't support you, which means the risk is all yours if we get sued as a result.** Here's where it gets interesting, and a little Machiavellian, for the Cop with a higher level of assertiveness. If you don't like the rules, the Cop will wonder aloud about the possibility of you not following them. Of course, rules are rules, and if the company ends up taking an EEOC charge based on your decision, the Cop is likely to have their conversations with you 100 percent documented.

   "Ladies and gentlemen of the jury, I did counsel the accused not to make the decision he made. But he did it anyway." Fear. Doubt. Uncertainty. Go ahead and try it. Feeling lucky? Didn't you just buy a new house? Seems risky to me.

   (Pro tip: This approach is best used when the Cop doesn't have as much leverage as they would like.)

4. **No, you can't do that because I need to get check-off approval on this decision.** A variant of the "risk is all yours" form of saying no, check-off approval is a hat-tip to the Cop asking their HR boss (or the boss of the person asking HR to say yes) to weigh in. The implied threat of this check-off approval play is that the next-level authority just bought a premium pontoon boat they couldn't afford and has little to no appetite for being unemployed in the next three years as a result.

   "Hi Don. Jerry wants to fire Monica. I don't think we should do it because <yadda, yadda, yadda>, but I told her I'd ask you if you think we should take that kind of risk."

(Pro Tips from the Cop's Playbook: 1) The Cop does the asking, 2) The Cop shares their opinion while asking for check-off, and 3) The Cop uses guiding language like "risk" in framing the decision the authority in question needs to make.)

You're dealing with a pro in getting a "no" from the Cop.

5. **No, you can't do that because if you do, I'll never forget this and try to end your career if I ever get the chance.** This is the nuclear option for the Cop. By the time things get to this point, the Cop has either worked through other options to get to "no" or sensed that they can't reason with you. With that in mind, they're willing to go down the "you'll be dead to me" road, which is off-putting to all but the most stubborn, powerful, and bullheaded corporate creatures.

Versions of this "I'm never going to forget this" moment with the Cop include:

"Really? I've giving you the best advice I can, and you're just going to discount it?"

"I've seen people make this type of decision. It didn't end well for them here."

"I'm not telling you that you can't go against my advice, I'm just telling you that if you do that, I can't guarantee you anything about the viability of your career at X." (Actually used by a Darth Vader of HR to me earlier in my HR career!!!!)

If you're a Cop in the 9 Faces of HR model, don't despair. There's always going to be a home for you.

The bigger question for the Cop is this—can you see change coming and mute some of the more dominant ways you face the outside world? If you can, you'll make people believe you are part of the solution. If you can't, you'll end up looking like a barrier rather than a partner.

20

The Rookie

I love to see a young girl go out and grab the world by the lapels. Life's a bitch. You've got to go out and kick ass.
—Maya Angelou

Meet Veronica, the Rookie

"Are you coming or not?"

Saturday nights were for the girls. At least that was the motto in the house Veronica lived in. She had connected with the other two girls through volunteer work in the 2016 Clinton campaign, and they had stretched to lease a house in the McCormick Row House District in the Lincoln Park area of Chicago.

"Go ahead and go, I'll catch up later. Got to get one thing out for work," Veronica shouted back after a thirty second delay. Saturday night at 9. seemed like a strange time to have to work. But Veronica wasn't working, she was waiting.

Earlier in the day, Veronica had submitted final work on a project she was working on at Bedazzled

Figure 20.1. Veronica the Rookie

Software. She had joined Bedazzled two years ago as a twenty-four-year old with a goal of becoming a CHRO by the time she was thirty. Working for a company focused on the human capital sector seemed to make sense from a learning perspective.

Two years in, she had already been promoted twice and was now a HRBP for the development group. One of the things she loved about working in HR at Bedazzled was the fact that the leaders seemed to really value and admire her work.

Veronica knew this project would blow them away. With access to developers, she had rigged up a tool to measure strength of internal networks and knowledge via analysis of email data. Her study had showed what she thought was true—many young professionals at Bedazzled were relied on in ways that transcended their total years of experience.

Veronica stared at her laptop screen. She had submitted the slides and her report to her boss and the CHRO at 3:00. It was now 9:15. Why hadn't she heard back?

The last two times she had submitted project work, she had heard back personally from the CHRO (a notorious workaholic) within two hours of sending.

Nothing. What was wrong with her work? No note from the CHRO. Not even an email from her boss. Six hours in.

Damn.

9:37. She picked up her phone to fire a text off to her boss to make sure she had seen the email.

Veronica reminded herself not to text like a millennial in need of a trophy.

Rookies: Can't Live with Them, Can't Live without Them

Veronica can easily be classified as the Rookie in the 9 Faces of HR model.

Rookies are early-career HR pros with a high ability to innovate, drive change, and add value. They're normally seen as bright, young stars within the modern HR practice. They tend to outshine their peers and even many mid-career HR pros with a mixture of aggressiveness, ambition, personal expectation, and delivery.

Large consulting firms (management consulting, accounting, and technology) base 90 percent of their staffing strategy on hiring the equivalent of the Rookie in their industries. They pump extensive resources into college recruiting machines designed to attract as many smart kids as they can to their organizations.

Once recruited and signed, the model for these consulting firms is pretty simple—up or out. Young professionals who do well get promoted, with many of the high performers becoming part of the succession plan at various levels of the organization over a ten-year period. Low performers either get fired or are left to stagnate at the entry-level as long as they perform at a base level.

Dealing with the Rookie in HR is an entirely different deal. Most HR shops don't do extensive college recruiting, so the Rookie appears in an entry-level hire as more of an accident than a strategic staffing plan. That's a good thing, right?

Not so fast, my friend.

You made an entry level HR hire. The Rookie shows up on day one, and you're happy you hired someone who's smart, goal oriented, and wants to do great work. Congrats! But be warned, *the clock is already ticking in week one related to the following expectations held by the Rookie*:

» **The Rookie isn't going to be happy with doing transactions very long.** Funny thing about those entry level jobs. They tend to require touching the transactional side of HR. The Rookie will tell you they're down with that, but by month four of what they're now terming "the situation," they're looking to off-load transactional responsibility onto weaker teammates, your receptionist, and whoever else is available to be run over. They're labeling this move "internal outsourcing."

» **The Rookie expects to work on meaningful projects.** If there's one thing the Rookie loves, it's access to the strategic side of HR. Be warned, once you give them the deck presented by the CHRO to the leadership team or board of directors at your company, they're going to have questions. They're going to want assignments related to some of those strategic areas. You'll say yes initially, and then remember that the Rookie's biggest career accomplishment is being named rush director for Delta Delta Delta.

» **The Rookie feels they deserve access to senior-level leaders.** How does your CHRO feel about drop-ins to their office? I only ask because true rookies will find a way to gain access to your boss (and your boss's boss for those of you in mega companies) if it's not provided institutionally. Your boss will casually mention during your one-on-one that Veronica (The Rookie) dropped by with a question on Tuesday. You'll want to transfer them to another building or, at least, provide coaching to "chill out," neither of which you'll be able to do without looking as old and threatened as one of the Golden Girls. Rookies are fun!

» **The Rookie won't be shy about destroying sleepy mid-level HR pros with their work.** If you're a HR shop of any size, The Rookie is going to start putting pressure on people who are above them in the org chart and are a little too comfortable. This may also be you, BTW. The Rookie will take every project (including the ones that have been assigned but people are just too busy to get to) and attempt to suck all the oxygen out of the room to show they're capable of great things. Some people in your HR shop will hate them as a result.

» **One promotion a year is the expectation of a true Rookie.** The Rookie has goals. The Rookie understands the reality— they're different than their early career peers, and as a result, paying dues the old-fashioned way doesn't really work for them.

In order to keep the Rookie, you'll need to promote them once a year, or at the very least, put them on a big project and bonus them a bit for their contributions. Yes, you can choose not to do these things. Yes, they'll build their portfolio with you a bit, and then they will bounce to another company if you don't put them on the fast track.

» **Brand matters to The Rookie, because they want to play for the Patriots, not the Browns.** There's a chance if you have the Rookie on your team that your employment brand and the reputation of your company is strong, mainly because the Rookie wouldn't have come to work for you if that wasn't the case. But, if your brand sucks and you just slopped into hiring the Rookie, you've got retention issues from day one. You'll be an organ donor to the rich because the Rookie will jump to a brand as soon as they have the resume to do it.

The message to those of you hiring at entry-level positions in your HR practices is clear. You should decide if you can live with the ambition of the Rookie. Don't be surprised that true Rookies in the 9 Faces of HR model want to be a CHRO by the time they're 30.

Embrace that ambition or screen them the hell out if you can't handle it.

Let's Check the DNA of The Rookie, Shall We?

Ambition. Expectation. A need for world-domination. These are a few of the things embedded deep in the DNA of the Rookie.

As the complexity and difficulty of the world becomes more apparent to them in their thirties, the Rookie moderates and relaxes their expectation and need for advancement and recognition. But the DNA markers of the Rookie are alive and well as they exit college and seek to join an HR team they can respect and, of course, one that respects them back.

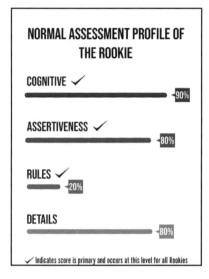

Figure 20.2. Scorecard for the Rookie

Primary DNA Characteristics of the Rookie

»   **High Cognitive/High Processing Speed.** No surprise here, the Rookie has high cognitive ability, and with it, the ability to juggle ten things at once. This processing speed means they can get the daily tasks of the entry-level HR job they are in completed in twenty hours per week. Bonus! High processing speed means The Rookie will likely attempt to finish the sentences of teammates and internal clients. They can't help themselves—you'll need to be their coach in this area.

»   **Assertiveness. Spoiler alert!** The Rookie has a high assertiveness score at the 80th percentile and above. Rookies fair better in most organizations when their assertiveness score it NOT above the 90th percentile, since a twenty-four-year old telling mid-career professionals they're wrong has a way of being not well received. Coaching is again required from you in this area. It's one thing to be assertive, it's another thing to run over teammates and clients in a public way. You'll need to encourage them to use a diary to express their plans for world domination, rather than overtly signaling it to anyone who is watching or listening.

» **Low Rules Orientation.** Low rules people love chaos. When things are flying around unresolved, the Rookie smells opportunity. Being comfortable with the freak show that exists in your company means an enterprising Rookie can take their pick of projects and find the ones with the best probability of strapping a SpaceX booster rocket to their career prospects.

Secondary DNA Characteristic of the Rookie

» **Detail Orientation.** Detail orientation of the Rookie can exist across a wide range within the 9 Faces of HR model. We'll talk more about a major trend involving detail orientation in young professional hiring next to wrap up our profile of the Rookie.

If Your See this Profile in an Early Career Candidate, Hire Them on the Spot

Here's a parting shot of our tour inside the mind of The Rookie. When hiring any entry level professional role, there's a behavioral profile that's emerging as the profile of choice across all industries. It's simple to spot and powerful as hell: Low Rules Orientation, High Detail Orientation.

Why is this simple profile so powerful? The combination of Low Rules, High Detail Orientation means someone likes the chaos of an unstructured situation and wants to create the solution (creativity and idea generation comes with that), but they also have the detail orientation necessary to execute on the plan.

Put simply: This candidate embraces chaos and loves to dream, but they are wired to actually deliver on what they dream up. This profile combination is powerful in early career hires, but it is also a desired profile combo at all levels of most modern organizations.

When's the last time you heard someone say, "You know, we really need more people who are perfectly satisfied with the way things are. Milking the cash cow part of our business should get us through the next thirty years."

RIP—Toys "R" Us, Circuit City, Borders, Zenith.

When evaluating the cost/benefit analysis of the Rookie, low rules/high details also presents a nice pressure release point. High detail orientation in a Rookie will likely cause that individual to be more patient with the transactional part of an entry-level HR role compared to a similar candidate with low- to mid-detail orientation.

Translation: The high details Rookie will give you more time to get them out of a role that involves transactions.

Good luck with your hiring of the Rookie profile.

Veronica is waiting for some positive feedback on a Saturday night.

Does HR Certification or an MBA Make Me More Desirable in HR?

In the economy of HR talent, there are buyers and sellers. Buyers are hiring executives at the C-level or CHROs/VPs of HR. Sellers are the candidates who want to work for them.

The Rookie is always the candidate with the most questions about how to improve their career prospects in the world of HR. This is to be expected as they're normally seen as bright, young stars within the modern HR practice. They tend to outshine their peers and even many mid-career HR pros with a mixture of aggressiveness, ambition, personal expectation, and delivery.

The ambition part is why they have more questions than any of the other 9 Faces of HR. Let's take a look at the two most common career questions Rookies have.

Does HR Certification Improve My Chances of Advancing Quicker?

Because I write frequently at *The HR Capitalist* and *Fistful of Talent*, Rookies hit me up at least a couple of times per month with a question like this: "I aspire to be a vice president of human resources one day, and I was wondering if I need a certification, like those offered by SHRM? How important is it in pursuing my career goal?"

The answer is pretty simple. To reach a goal of becoming a VP of HR, you'll need to be among the best at what you do as an HR professional who rises through the HR rep, manager, and director levels in any organization. The HR discipline is filled with great VP examples on both sides of this question—those who have certification and those who don't. You've got to be progressive, business-savvy, and results-oriented, and you can do that without certification as many have.

So, here's the bottom line from my perspective: Certification is valuable to everyone, but common sense dictates that the economic and career path value is greater for those who are early in their careers. If you are at the HR manager level or below and can make the time to pursue certification, do it now. You'll differentiate yourself from the herd, whether you plan on staying forever in your *Fortune* 500 HR shop or intend to switch jobs and companies in the next couple of years. Certification is often used as a "resume sorter" by many companies when it comes time to hire their next HR manager, HR director, or VP of HR.

Certification isn't generally required to promote or get a better job in your company. That said, if a significant portion of companies use it to evaluate candidate criteria, it makes sense to have it. The quicker you gain the necessary experience at the rep, manager, and director level, the quicker you'll get to your goal of being a VP of HR. Expand your pool of opportunity if you have the time and resources to pursue certification.

Is Getting an MBA or Master's Degree Worth the Time and Money?

I'm also fortunate to hear from VPs of HR and HR directors as they hit the recruiting trail to fill positions on their HR teams. When it comes to the value of advanced degrees in those HR searches, here's a telling email I received from a VP of HR recently:

> Would love to know your opinion on a trend I am seeing as
> I'm screening HR manager candidates. I used to encourage
> HR undergrads to pursue their master's in business admin-
> istration (MBA) instead of a masters in HR. I felt it held
> more value for businesses and was a tough program that
> would advance them in ways a specialized degree couldn't.
> I am shocked at the number of candidates I am seeing with
> an MBA or MA in HR. The result for me is that I am losing
> respect for the MBA! I mean, if so many people can get
> one, is it really a tough program? Does it really demonstrate
> anything special anymore?

I obviously have to lead with a Groucho Marx quote here—"I'd
never belong to any club that would have me as a member."

I think the advice they provided is still relevant, and if it's any
consolation, lots of young HR pros followed their advice, right?
Now they're pissed off that people like me won't get out of the way
fast enough, and in a cocktail of following this advice and having
time on their hands, they've got more degrees than they have jobs. I
say this as someone with three degrees, including an MBA. But I'm
Gen X—now a veteran of HR.

The trend identified is obviously related to an explosion in the
accessibility and availability of the MBA. Distance learning and a
multitude of options has made the MBA tag a bit easier to gather,
which I think means we've got to evaluate what the candidates are
actually presenting in a couple of different ways:

1. **Where did they pick up the MBA, and did they actually have to work hard to achieve it?** Traditional programs
   where you have to spend time in class still rule in my eyes—
   that commitment, along with the interaction that occurs
   when you have to work in groups with other humans, is still
   the most important thing. That being said, there are a lot of
   online MBA programs that work the hell out of people. Of

course, there are a lot of diploma mills as well, which is why some people feel the MBA scene is watered down.

Good rule of thumb: any school with a directional name without reference to a state or city is a problem. Southeast Missouri? Sounds legit to me. Southeastern University? Wait, Southeastern where?

2. **The most important thing related to the MBA is what they learned and how it's changed them.** With that in mind, some of the interview process has to go after what they learned from the MBA program and how they applied it. Additionally, how has it changed them? If someone really took the MBA and ran with it, it should result in a change related to how they viewed their job. Do they have a portfolio of work in their life as an HR pro that was influenced by the MBA? No portfolio means they checked off a box and really didn't apply it. Existence of a portfolio means it changed their worldview, and the young HR pro is now looking to create a work product that's fundamentally stronger and regularly applied.

Young HR pros like the Rookie want to rule the world. With that in mind, they should chase certification and advanced degrees as early as possible if they have the time and the means. But certification and degrees on paper without being able to show the value it's helped you create in your career is just a resume sorter.

Hey Rookies! Start creating portfolios of your value-added work if you want to prove your HR chops and promotability.

21

The Clerk

Hey, You know they're all the same
You know you're doing better on your own so don't buy in
Live right now, Just be yourself
It doesn't matter if that's good enough for someone else
–*The Middle* by Jimmy Eat World from *Bleed American*

Freddie Could Go Either Way

"Whatever you think boss."

It was true. As he was fond of saying, he was ambivalent to the decision that was about to be made. Freddie was an HR coordinator at GroceryRunner.com. He had been with the grocery shopping service for two years in the corporate office, working for Carol, the HR manager in charge of serving the technology division. He did what most HR coordinators did, handling the transactions, onboarding, and generally all incoming inquiries so Carol could hose down the daily fires caused by employees.

Figure 21.1. Freddie the Clerk

Jill, the CHRO at GroceryRunner, had done one of her infamous drop-ins and asked his opinion about whether the code competition, a recognition and employee relations tactic of sorts, should be shut down.

Freddie never missed Davidson College after graduating four years ago. Truth be told, he regretted not doing the reasonable thing and attending UNC-Charlotte. He would have one-fourth of the student loans to pay off and have had a better time. He was actually influenced by the fact that Steph Curry went to Davidson, which at twenty-six years old seemed a lot less logical than it did at eighteen.

"I'm asking you what you think, Freddie." Jill said. There was an edge in her voice.

There it was. Jill wasn't going to let go, and Carol was in Croatia on a goodwill trip to one of GroceryRunner's offshore tech centers. Freddie glanced over Jill's shoulder at the digital display. It was 10:30 p.m. in Zagreb, Carol had her sleep blinders on, and was already in an Ambien-induced sleep. Not that it mattered, because this was the normal Jill playbook—put more responsibility on the minions than their title would suggest they had, chain of command be dammed. They called her "drive-by Jill." Still, everyone respected and loved her.

"If I was on the debate team, I could take either side. Kill it, or don't kill it." The words seemed weak coming out of his mouth. He kind of wanted to take them back halfway out, but they were already done.

"Math, Freddie. Make the call based on what you do best."

There were forty people in the HR department, and Jill knew he was carrying a stats minor from Davidson. She had dropped emails to him before asking for analysis of things she was working on, always copying Carol. The first time he gave her some analysis, she took thirty minutes to show him how he should package the analysis for the C-level.

"I think the utilization of the program is understated. There are five power users in a division of 500 hoodies. They make it look like 10 percent of the function is active, but it's not true. For the money we're spending, we should shut it down. It's been a year." That felt a bit too direct. Jill smiled at him as she pulled her arm down from his cubicle. Somebody was about to have their pet project killed.

"That's what I felt, but I didn't have the stats to back it up. I'll probably ask Carol to have you pull the numbers, so don't be surprised when that happens. I'll tell her we talked and make it okay for you." Jill said.

Freddie knew a lot about the mesh point of data and employee behavior at GroceryRunner. After all, he is the Clerk, and while he knows a lot, you're probably going to have to ask if you want the scoop.

Welcome to the Middle, the Home of the Clerk

The Clerk is an early-career HR pro with mid-range ability to innovate, drive change, and add value. What makes The Clerk reside at the intersection of center street and median avenue? The following things come to mind:

» **The Clerk doesn't have as much ambition as the Rookie.** The Rookie wants to be a CHRO by the time they're thirty. The Clerk is thinking about a new monitor sometime next year, and they were wondering if they could get an Adobe Cloud subscription, so they could tinker around with their reports. #squadgoals

» **The Clerk isn't really sure what they want to do with their life.** HR seems okay. That's as far as they can take you related to their commitment to the field. Odds are, The Clerk doesn't have an HR degree and kind of just walked into this whole HR thing without a plan (see chapter 2). They are intrigued by this whole employee relations thing though because there's a high likelihood they report to an HR manager or HRBP who's always interviewing someone in a he said/she said free-for-all.

» **The Clerk always knows more than they tell you about.** They're likely the systems admin and power user for the various systems you use and care about in HR, and they've quietly built up a sizeable knowledge base about the guts of human capital in your company. Unlike the Machine (which we'll profile next), the Clerk doesn't need command and control over process. They just want to be in the know, which ultimately makes them a great candidate for a succession plan to HR manager once you have an opening and they have the requisite experience.

» **The Clerk doesn't see things in black and white.** The world view of the Clerk is based on shades of gray, and they seek out data first when deciding their stance on any internal issue. You say that the offer point for position X is way too low? The Clerk is not only looking for external data, they are cutting data about incumbent retention with similar offer points. They don't take a big bite out of what you're selling, preferring to sit back, let some data points and conversations with others roll in, and then decide for themselves.

The Clerk is sneaky in their knowledge and aptitude of HR. They don't necessarily have the deep goals or the ambition of the Rookie, but they've got the ability to be more than a coordinator-level at your company.

Let's Check the DNA of the Clerk, Shall We?

Since we're profiling an early career HR pro with less ability to innovate than the Rookie, you might think we're headed straight to the high rules side of the house. You'd be wrong. While we're headed in that direction as we profile the Clerk, we're stopping way short of the destination you had in mind.

The Clerk is best described as The Fixer in training. While The Clerk has to respect the details necessary to handle the transactional side of an early stage career in HR, they've got a distinct behavioral profile that offers balance in ways similar to The Fixer.

The Rookie wants to rule the world. As you'll soon see, the Machine (our last early career profile coming up next) wants to be the system. The Clerk's not really sure what they want to be in HR when they grow up.

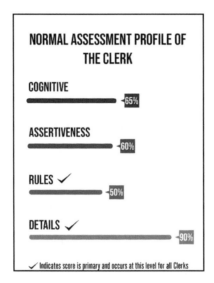

Figure 21.2. Scorecard for the Clerk

Primary DNA Characteristics of The Clerk

» **High Detail Orientation.** Members of your HR team who are naturals for The Clerk role all have one thing in common—high detail orientation. As we've shared elsewhere in this book, high detail orientation is highly sought after in the marketplace for young talent across all professions. The Clerk has a focus on details, is organized, and generally doesn't miss tasks. Unlike others with high detail orientation, The Clerk doesn't seek to be defined by organizational skills. They have too much interest in other things to be defined in that manner.

» **Mid-Level Rules Orientation.** After confirming high detail orientation, rules orientation is the key to identifying the Clerk. Unlike the Rookie (low rules) and the Machine (high rules), the Clerk's mid-range rules score means they won't view the world of work and HR from an "absolute" point of view. This sets The Clerk up nicely for a career after a transactional role, with the normal point of progression as an HR manager with a client group of employees. The key to the mid-level rules marker is that it unlocks the ability of the clerk to grow from an employee relations perspective. As we illustrated with the Fixer, this balanced view of what's necessary (rules) vs. what's possible (no rules) is the key to successful client group generalist work.

Secondary DNA Characteristics of The Clerk

» **Assertiveness.** While the details and rules markers are mandatory, Clerks in the 9 Faces of HR model can have a wide range of assertiveness. It's fair to say that the amount of assertiveness dictates which career direction Clerks go—if they are career minded at all. Lower assertiveness means the Clerk may be well placed or will seek out a supervisory or managerial role in functions like payroll, while mid-range to higher assertiveness points to the HR manger role often held by the Fixer persona.

» **Cognitive/High Processing Speed.** Not to be a broken record, but more cognitive power is always helpful and, if present, points the career-minded Clerk to the Fixer role.

4 Ways to Determine If a Clerk Can Be Your Next HR Manager

Career-pathing for the Clerk in any HR function of size and scale is not only desired, it's critical. Sure, you might promote the Rookie to

HR manager, but they're going to be tired of that and asking what the next step is in under a year.

That's why you need to know whether the Clerk is promotable. Even if you run an HR shop with two or three total employees, your career path and ability to leave and take another job on good terms may depend on the Clerk's ability to be promoted to the next level.

You already know that the Clerk has high detail and mid-range rule orientations (primary characteristics) and those characteristics are acceptable in an HR manager position. Now you need to test their processing speed and assertiveness in the following ways to determine if they are promotable.

1. **Make them responsible for making a departmental decision of some magnitude.** Jill did this in our example at the start of this chapter. They've likely got access to the data you need, so hit them with a situation that matters, tell them to research it, and come back to you (and potentially the rest of the team) with a recommendation. You'll learn a lot through this exercise about how they think.

2. **Give them their first employee relations quagmire to sort through.** Start with something basic, like attendance. The next time you get an incoming distress call from a manager for an attendance issue with a secondary variable (family situation, addiction, etc.), provide some prep for the Clerk and have them ride shotgun with the manager. Employee relations is going to be a big part of the next job. If it satisfies and interests them, you have a likely fit.

3. **Have the Clerk herd the cats when it comes to vendor selection.** You're going to select an external partner in area x, so why not put The Clerk in charge of all aspects of that project? You'll see how they handle internal clients (the rest of your HR team and non-HR people who need to be involved), how they think, how they present findings and thoughts, and more.

4. **Put them in charge of a micro-area across all HR operations.** This is a great option for bigger shops. If you're in a company with 1,000 or more employees, make the Clerk the go-to person in an area that's broken, like leave of absence, compensation requests, etc. Putting them in charge means they run it all—any request in the area comes to them. Have them install processes together, handle it all, and report the status at least once a month. You'll learn more about their capability to do process improvement by using them this way.

The Clerk's not sure what they want in their career. The smart HR leader is always evaluating who's on the bench and capable of promotion to the mid-level. You love the Rookie, but their ambition comes with strings attached. Don't forget about the Clerk. They might just be the Rookie without high assertiveness and naked ambition, which means they'll likely stick in the next role longer than the Rookie if they're a good match.

22

The Machine

Never send a human to do a machine's job.
—Agent Smith (Hugo Weaving) in *The Matrix* (1999)

Meet Brenda, the Machine

"IBS is nothing to play around with, my friend."

Brenda wasn't sure how she got here, but she was pretty sure she was in hell. Chuck had just plopped down in a seat at the entrance to her cubicle. She remembered that another employee had pulled the chair out of a makeshift conference room the HR team had established in the file room—and left it by her cube.

Brenda tried to tell her HR manager at JS Gilbert that using the file room for meetings was a bad idea due to security protocol. She was overridden because of the fact that all the conference rooms were converted into offices or more cubes. Yes, they worked at a commercial real estate firm.

Figure 22.1. Brenda the Machine

Now, she'd give up all that security to not have to listen to Chuck talk about his Irritable Bowel Syndrome (IBS). He sought her out to inquire about co-pays for a doctor's visit on the topic. Of course, it had led to more. The worst topics always lead to more.

Brenda had learned to look back at her screen just enough to get people like Chuck to realize the conversation was probably over without offending them. Soon, Chuck was gone.

"Do you have the leave of absence form you can shoot over to me?"

Finally, someone looking for service the way Brenda liked it—via Glip, the company's internal messaging app. The company had Slack at one time, but Ring Central had come in with a big suite of Telecom products, and Glip was their current version of Slack.

On the other side of the Glip conversation was Joanie. Joanie was a customer service rep at JS Gilbert and a serial leave taker. In the past five years, she'd been out on LOA at least four times. Brenda knew through conversations she'd heard around the HR wing that Joanie was viewed as a low performer, but the LOAs had frozen her manager from really doing anything related to her performance.

Nothing made Brenda happier than crossing something off her list—except crossing something off that had never been put on the list due to it being handled quickly. She pinged Joanie back with the form in question and thought about how much better HR would run if everyone would use the technology that was available.

As Brenda added the already sent LOA form to her Outlook Tasks and marked the task complete, she thought about whether she should give an early warning to Joanie's manager or the HR manager for that client group that another LOA was in the works. Her first thought was no because the manager being a complete jerk, which was quickly confirmed and rationalized by the professional cloak of the need for confidentiality.

"Did you know John makes $17 per hour? WTF!"

Ashley was such a piece of work. Brenda still remembered the new hire orientation they were both a part of seven years ago. Brenda was a new hire in accounts payable, where she still worked. They shared a common love of all things Brad Paisley, and they routinely ate lunch together.

Brenda got random texts from Ashley at least three times per week. They were usually about celebrity gossip but occasionally included tidbits of work rumors. Brenda had learned the hard way these were fishing expeditions seeking to confirm information via her position to access HR info. Brenda decided to deflect in her text back to Ashley: "No. Did you know Chuck is dealing with IBS?"

Brenda didn't think much about sharing Chuck's personal struggles with IBS because she had heard him telling a table of five about his struggles last week in the break room. There's only one Chuck, she thought.

"LOL. What does he make? Later."

Ashley had successfully been deflected. She knew better than to test Brenda. As Brenda toggled back to email, she checked the human resource management system (HRMS). John in accounts receivable made $16 an hour.

Brenda had a name for dealing with things like IBS, a serial LOA candidate, and a friend pumping her for salary info.

Brenda called that "Tuesday."

Welcome to the Life of the Machine

Someday, automation will reign supreme, and if we're lucky, our technology overlords will have established a Universal Basic Income (UBI) to fund our Netflix, fast casual dining, and Fortnite needs. Until that Nirvana arrives, the Machine stands ready to execute your HR transactions with order and excellence.

The Machine is an early career HR pro who has low ability and willingness to innovate, drive change, and add incremental value you don't expect. They can generally be found in titles like HR assistant, HR coordinator, and a variety of other titles that suggest, "I'm taking care of the details, process, and transactions so you don't have to."

The Machine likes things to be in order. Things the Machine has been known to say in HR departments around the world include:

» "It's not that hard, people."
» "Open enrollment is my tax season."
» "You should talk to your HR manager about that—that's above my pay grade." (Used when some walk-in starts sharing an employee relations situation with lots of messy grey areas that's likely to take twelve hours of interviews to resolve).
» "We need more rules about what people can put in the HR suggestion box."
» "I've always enjoyed the smell of payroll in the morning."

The fact that the Machine is coded as an entry-level persona is complicated. HR employees can start here and move up if they have the right stuff, but it's also not uncommon for the early career HR pro to start here and remain in the entry-level of the HR industry for a decade or more.

If that happens, the Machine has likely found the only home in HR they'll be happy, or successful, in.

Let's Check the DNA of The Machine, Shall We?

You might think that being defined as having low ability and willingness to innovate, drive change, or add value is a bad thing all the time. You'd be wrong—look around any HR shop of any size and you'll see people who have a natural pre-disposition to making sure that the dirty work gets done and the trains run on time.

It all comes down to the role you have those people in. If you have the Machine in a role charged with operational excellence and making sure a pre-defined operations manual is executed, they can help you win. If you have them in a role where they are forced to deal with heavy ambiguity, it's not going to go well. Let's take a look at the DNA of the Machine.

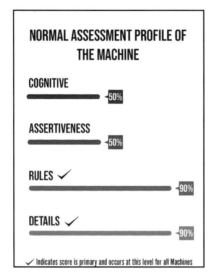

Figure 22.2. Scorecard for the Machine

Primary DNA Characteristics of the Machine

» **High Rules Orientation.** Everything the Machine does is driven by a need to find and deliver on a set of rules that sets the expectation for their work life. If you have an HR operations manual, they're set. They'll follow it to a "T" and tell you when the rules don't cover situations they encounter. As they find common circumstances not covered by rules, you'll have the need to help drive the structure they crave. Some versions of The Machine will drive the formulation of new rules, while some simply want to be told what the rules are. The strength of the rules score, along with the secondary characteristic of assertiveness, drives their approach and ability in this area.

» **High Detail Orientation**. Individuals with the Machine persona have a high need to organize their lives. This means the Machine rarely misses a follow-up or a task they promised to do because they have engineered their lives with a high degree of organization using lists, technology, and memory to manage details better than most in your HR practice.

Note that in our intro, Brenda created and checked off a task that had already been completed. That's the Machine when it comes to detail orientation. #NatureOverNuture

Secondary DNA Characteristics of The Machine

» **Assertiveness.** The Machine can have a high range of assertiveness. In order to be the Machine, high rules and detail orientation are mandatory. Assertiveness is a secondary characteristic of the machine. Low assertiveness Machines are destined to stay in transactional roles for a long time. High assertiveness Machines have the opportunity to promote up in traditional organizations, as this trait is needed to deal with common situations at the HR manager, director, and HRBP level.

» **Cognitive/High Processing Speed.** Also secondary to the persona of The Machine, more processing speed on the cognitive front is always nice to have. But it won't be used to innovate unless that innovation is about getting more people to follow rules, which is the opposite of the type of change most organizations need. #Process

It always comes down to the match of the job/employee in the 9 Faces of HR model. If you hate HR transactions, you probably need a Machine in your life.

Do's and Don'ts for Interacting with Your Machine

As with any piece of technology, there are things the Machine is capable of and things that will cause an error message. Used properly, the Machine is a key component of any HR function. Error messages happen when you don't use the Machine towards what it was built for.

Here's a simple operator's manual for the Machine:

> **Do:** *Load up your Machine with volume.* The Machine loves large batches of simple transactions and processes. Load it up—the six sigmas at the factory load tested the Machine's capability, and they rarely showed stress with a high volume of simple tasks.

> **Don't:** *Try to use the Machine for something other than its intended purpose.* You want research done on performance management? You didn't bring the Machine aboard for that. The warning label told you not to try this.

> **Do:** *Make your Machine a key part in implementing new HR technology.* The Machine loves technology and adores its ability to make people follow a process. Nothing satisfies the Machine more than digging into a manual and figuring out how to make base HR tech work smoothly.

> **Don't:** *Expect your Machine to do training on new HR technology.* You might be tricked into thinking the Machine will enjoy talking about the new technology they configured. You would be wrong. Humans are messy, and your Machine would rather deal with the tech.

> **Do:** *Put the Machine in a private area designed for getting things done.* The biggest show of respect you can give the

Machine is putting them in a private area. You're saying "I see you," and giving the Machine what they need. Well played.

Don't: *Put the Machine in a high traffic area where people with problems approach them because they are the face of HR.* As we mentioned with HR tech, the Machine likes systems, details, data, and transactions. You know what they don't like? The people. They could do without the people.

Do: *Make the Machine the reports expert.* They like data and they love the control that being a reporting expert provides them. By making them responsible for reports, you're putting them in charge of an area they can thrive in. They'll never forget you for this.

Don't: *Take the Machine along to the leadership team meeting, and give them a "stretch" assignment of presenting the monthly report.* They're going to melt down if you do this. All the "what if this" and "what if that" questioning in the room is enough to send them over the edge.

Every HR leader needs a Machine in their life. Find the model that best fits you, put them in a corner with max privacy, and don't expect them to do anything they're not good at. One day, automation will take these jobs away from us, and you'll miss the unique stylings of the Machine.

A.I.'s "Gaydar" Is Better Than Yours, But That's Probably Going to Go Horribly Wrong

The biggest risk to The Machine in the 9 Faces of HR model is job loss due to automation.

So let's talk about artificial intelligence (A.I.) and machine learning, shall we?

I'm a straight white guy, which is equal parts boring and pedestrian. Because we all tribe together, that means the majority of my friends are straight.

This is where I should insert a note to tell you that I have friends who aren't straight, and that I'd make a great VP of diversity, even though I'm white, male, and straight. I'm not going to do that. Instead I'll let you soak in the irony that non-diverse people love to insert context here to make them seem more diverse.

You know what a lot of my straight friends think they have? Laser-focused "gaydar." "Gaydar" is defined by Wikipedia as follows:

> **Gaydar** (a portmanteau of gay and radar) is a colloquialism referring to the intuitive ability of a person to assess others' sexual orientations as gay, bisexual, or heterosexual. Gaydar relies almost exclusively on non-verbal clues and LGBT stereotypes. These include the sensitivity to social behaviors and mannerisms; for instance, acknowledging flamboyant body language, the tone of voice used by a person when speaking, overtly rejecting traditional gender roles, a person's occupation, and grooming habits.

The only thing that I would add to that definition is that almost everyone I know believes their "gaydar" is 100 percent accurate, which can't be correct. What they're missing is the false negatives, which is to say they can make the "easy" calls, but they never know all the times their "gaydar" failed them.

You know whose "gaydar" is really good? According to CNBC, apparently Artificial Intelligence:

> Artificial Intelligence (AI) can now accurately identify a person's sexual orientation by analyzing photos of their face, according to new research. The Stanford University study, which is set to be published in the Journal of Personality and Social Psychology and was first reported in The Economist, found that machines had a far superior "gaydar" when compared to humans.
>
> The machine intelligence tested in the research could correctly infer between gay and straight men 81 percent of the time, and 74 percent of the time for women. In contrast, human judges performed much worse than the sophisticated computer software, identifying the orientation of men 61 percent of the time and guessing correctly 54 percent of the time for women.

It's been said that technology and data do not discriminate. But A.I. changes all of that because it learns as it goes along, which means that A.I. is going to start discriminating—in this case, against the LGBTQA+ community. It won't be called discrimination, however—it will be called "opportunity maximization." Here are three ways A.I. will ultimately learn to discriminate against the LGBTQA+ and non-LGBTQA+ communities as a result of the learning:

1. **A hiring manager spends large amounts of time watching Fox News and is a member of a church that would be considered less than friendly to the LGBTQA+ community.**

Since A.I. can now identify who's gay, it learns over time that LGBTQA+ career outcomes are never good with this type of hiring manager, so it stops feeding a gay man or woman jobs with said type of hiring manager.

2. **An image scan of LinkedIn shows that the managerial ranks of a company include an industry-low number of LGBTQA+ employees.** As a result, A.I. fails to deliver the company's managerial jobs to LGBTQA+ candidates as a priority, instead showing them on the eighth page of Google for jobs search results.

3. **A gay hiring manager has a track record of success for hiring and promoting high performing LGBTA+ community members—which is a good thing.** BUT, the search results delivered to this manager always prioritize the type of candidate who has outperformed expectations with him in the past—as a result, he sees a disproportionate amount of LGBTQA+ resumes when compared to the marketplace.

Are these examples of discrimination? Some would say no, because numbers and data don't lie—these are just examples of A.I. simply trying to maximize business results based on the increasing treasure trove of data that will come online over time.

In maximizing business results, however, A.I. takes opportunities away from LGBTQA+ and non-LGBTQA+ candidates. And this is only one example—take any protected or non-protected class and A.I will be able to identify the segmentation.

Don't believe that A.I can learn to discriminate? Google "Amazon Recruiting A.I." to learn how Amazon had to unplug an A.I.-based recruiting project when the machines penalized resumes that included the word "women's," as in "women's chess club captain." Amazon's A.I also downgraded graduates of two all-women's colleges as it churned through ten years of data, which (spoiler alert) showed men dominating the tech industry.

The "gaydar" of A.I. is strong. What wins as a result? Business results and outcomes or equal opportunity?

We shall see. Don't take FTEs out of your HR budget just yet based on the promise of A.I. and machine learning.

And yes, I'm aware that statement will come back to haunt me when the machines take over, they do a Google search on me, and, based on this statement, opt to put me in charge of global leave of absence (LOA) processes.

Turns out, that process is so bad, the machines won't even touch it.

23

Your Future Boss Thinks You Suck!

Is there some reason my coffee isn't here?
Has she died or something?
—Miranda Priestly (Meryl Streep) in *The Devil Wears Prada*
(2006)

"Where are we at with the openings in software development?"

If you remember this quote from our first chapter, give yourself a gold star. This quote came from Ed, the new CEO at GridLoad (put there by the controlling private equity firm) to Jenn, our Atlanta-based HR leader.

This question is not an invitation to list what's been done. It's a test.

Put on a helmet kids, because I'm about to give you some tough love.

Your Future Boss Thinks You Suck

At some point in the future, all of you reading this book are going to get a new boss. Most of you will have five to ten new bosses across the rest of your career, which is reflective of how chaotic work is for our generation and the general pace of change.

Some of those new bosses are going to have manageable expectations. But it's important to note that many of them are going to expect new things out of you, and they generally won't be that concerned with your feelings.

Many of the new bosses are going to expect you to be great in the way you do HR. The problem with that? Their definition of great is going to be different than yours, and their definition is the only one that counts.

Here's how your interactions with a new boss who expects you to be great are going to go:

1. **The new boss comes in and things appear fine.** This is called the "honeymoon" period. All parties are getting to know each other, and your new boss is forming opinions of what they've got related to talent on the team. There are lunches, light meetings, and, hell, even some jokes!

2. **You're presented with a challenge, and you do what you do, and what you have always done.** For Jenn in our first chapter, it was finding software development talent. She did what she has always done, which is to post far and wide and pray that those postings would be effective. Note that she didn't do more than she's always done in this area. It was out of her comfort zone, and what she had done previously had always been enough.

3. **The new boss expresses on some level that you'll need to think differently to meet their expectations.** How your new boss frames this request depends on the challenge, but it generally follows a "what else you got?," "I need more," or "go figure it out," conversational vibe.

4. **The new boss doesn't tell you what "more" looks like but will tell you if they're impressed by what you're doing.** That's why they're the boss. If they have to tell you what to do, they're not sure why they need you on the team. They won't tell you what to do, but they will compliment you if you're on the right track and if you keep them updated and tell them what you're doing.

5. **Silence is dangerous. Long stretches of silence are generally accompanied by you being fired or someone else being hired above you.** The most dangerous thing you can do with a new boss is not engage. If you accept silence and refuse to get in front of the relationship, that's you doing what you've always done. Organizational change usually follows long periods of silence.

You're on the clock with any new boss—both as an HR leader and a line HR pro. Whether you report to a CEO as an HR leader or a new VP of HR as a line HR pro, you're being tested. You have to play offense, which means you gotta rock it. No whining.

Doing what you've always done is dangerous. Let's talk next about why you're so comfortable with the status quo.

I've Been Doing It This Way for Years and No One's Ever Complained

I know. Things were fine before the new boss came along. You're not sure why you have to change, and it generally seems s***ty. I'm not here to argue with how you feel. I'm just here to tell you that most of us will have at least one new boss who's a lot like Ed was with Jenn at GridLoad. Your cadence with that new boss is going to feel almost exactly how I outlined it above—if you look closely.

The danger is when you don't make a move to get in front it. When the new boss comes in and immediately wonders if you suck at HR, it's not an automatic death sentence. You can adjust to the new expectation and perhaps even learn along the way. Let's talk about the reasons why some of you won't adjust when the new boss with different demands and opinions shows up on the scene:

» **Confrontation comes with change. Some of you aren't great at confrontation.**

As we moved through the personas in the 9 Faces of HR, we identified some HR types who are always high assertive—the Judge and the Assassin. For the rest of you, assertiveness is more variable, which means you may not have the natural stomach for the change that needs to happen. To react to the new boss with higher expectations, you'll have to be assertive in changing your day-to-day routine. While that's hard enough, it's only the tip of the iceberg. Reinventing how you are doing HR also comes with confrontation of others—vendors, the people you manage on your HR team, and the managers and employees in the client groups you support. If you're low to mid assertive, don't give in. You can do this—you'll just need to be at the top end of your assertiveness scale for a long period of time. Awareness that you'll avoid needed confrontation and adjusting that behavior is the first step to winning with a new boss.

» **Your client group seems to dig what you do!**

Rationalization 101. Your people love you. Your customers love you. Things are going great. Who is this person to come in and judge how you do your job? I've seen it a hundred times. The indignation. You're the expert, right? People rely on you, and you've been told that you're the best HR pro they've ever worked with. I think those people are right. You're awesome. I also think that your new boss has different needs, and the clock just started ticking when they had their first session with you. The honeymoon will be over soon. Be indignant for a day, maybe two, then get to it.

» **Sidetracks are available to help you rationalize.**

The rationalization isn't over with the aforementioned "people love my work." You'll be hit with other rationalizations like the popular, "what about them?" (you'll claim other people aren't being judged in the same way by the new boss) and "my tools suck" (shout out to the fact you have imperfect tools and team resources to help you get things done). Of course, none of these sidetracks matter. Many of you know this because you've dabbled in leadership development as HR pros and will label the feelings as excuses by the third time you feel them. The rest of you should read this section eleven times.

» **You've got a life. This "change" stuff interrupts your flow!**

If you choose to fully engage your new boss, you're basically starting a new job. Sometimes that's tough to get your head around, as your surroundings haven't changed—same people in your office, same desk, same Mexican restaurant on Wednesday, etc. A new boss is going to interrupt that flow. To fully engage them, you'll need to make some choices and sacrifices. There's going to be occasions where face time is available late in the day or early in the evening, or there's going to be digital interactions late and over the weekend, all of which can impact the routine you've settled into with your family, loved ones, and the thing we call "life." Not engaging in these ways is a choice some of you will make. You'll point to work/life balance, tenure, and a bunch of other stuff that really doesn't matter. The new boss with high expectations and doubt related to your capabilities is actually a new job. If you don't realize that, there's a chance the thing you call your job might just be an extended severance period. Wake up.

When the new boss rolls in, you're going to feel these things as an HR pro. Some of you will internalize the sidetracks and rationalization and not push through to embrace the change. Many of you will survive doing nothing. Some of you won't. Good luck rolling the dice. If you're ready to engage, let's talk about a simple playbook available to make sure you're on the same page as the new boss.

How to Manage the New Boss as an HR Pro

There's a lot of mystery with a new boss who is in "evaluation mode." Many new bosses will come in, watch, ask questions, and provide little direct input about what they would like to see. This reality is more distinct with director and VP of HR positions than it is with line HR positions.

Regardless if your new boss is an HR leader (for my HR managers and levels below) or a C-level (for my director/VP of HR brothers and sisters), there's a path you can take to eliminate the mystery and extract actual feedback from your new boss. Feedback from the new boss is a gift. Feedback sets the performance curve you'll be graded on. Feedback co-opts the new boss into a partnership with you to build something good, if not great.

Your goal should be to manage up instead of waiting. Remember, silence is deadly when it comes to the new boss. Of course, managing up often means you have to do some work you weren't doing before. It's also going to feel pretty confrontational for my low to mid-assertive buckaroos out there.

Here's my playbook for how HR pros can manage the new boss:

» **Ask the new boss what they'd like to see.** As simple as it seems, you could ask, right? This involves brainstorming with your new boss after you've asked the broad question. Effective follow-ups to keep the brainstorming going include:

> › "What were the most valuable things your last HR team did to impact the business?"
> › "What have you seen in your first month related to HR that you'd like to focus on?"
> › "If you had to rank order the things HR does in importance to you, what would you rank first? Second?"
> › "What do you like about me?"

I'm kidding about the last one. There's nothing worse than asking that question and hearing, "Well, you certainly seem to have a clean office. I like the color of your Camry as well."

» **All joking aside, be ready for anything once you ask these questions and keep your sensitivity low.** Some new bosses will be reserved, some will unload in a way that will make you feel less than stellar. Keep your eyes on the prize—if you ask the question and they talk, you win.

» **Become more project focused.** You can use project work as a stand-alone or a natural next step to asking your new boss what they'd like to see. Project work means improvement, enhancements, and moving your HR practice forward in addition to managing your day-to-day work.

» **Being actively engaged with projects aligned with your new boss's view of the HR world is key.** Figure out what's important to them and then chase improvements in these areas. Cover the project status with the new boss periodically to show progress and get more feedback.

» **Become more metric and reporting focused.** Data rules in today's world, and chances are you don't have enough of it in your HR function. Start reporting in a cadence that makes sense for you, but once you start reporting, don't skip due dates. Scheduling a quick meeting with your new boss to cover the trends is a great way to find out what's most important to them— they'll tell you what they think is missing.

» **Don't get co-opted into other people's situations with the new boss.** In any leadership change, there's going to be winners and losers. Your goal is to follow this playbook and be one of the winners. In your HR role, it's likely you'll be an outlet for other people's frustrations. You've got to listen and give them a playbook that's similar to this. You can't get co-opted into any else's negative situation. Stay above the fray here. Don't agree with negative opinions. Instead, give them tools to manage the relationship and don't get dragged in.

"Where are we at with <insert any request for status from a new boss>?"

If you hear this type of question from a new boss—like Jenn did at GridLoad—understand that it's usually a test or a call for change. Most of you reading this will have multiple new bosses as an HR pro in the next ten years. Understand the risk and be ready to roll with the punches. You're capable of surviving the new boss who initially thinks you suck, but only if you engage and treat it like a new job.

24

Staying Alive: Using The 9 Faces of HR to Protect and Build your Career

The question isn't what are we going to do?
The question is what aren't we going to do?
—Ferris Bueller (Matthew Broderick) in
Ferris Bueller's Day Off (1986)

The best thing about the 9 Faces of HR isn't the cool titles for the personas or guessing which face some of your HR teammates and friends are. Those things are fun, but the most important thing can be summed up in one word.

Awareness.

Understanding who you are as an HR pro—what your motivations are, what you do best, and what you subconsciously avoid is an incredible opportunity in finding more satisfaction in your HR career. Once you have that understanding, the next thing you need is *honesty*. You're going to have to be honest with yourself in understanding that your internal behavioral DNA not only drives your HR success, but also your HR failures.

If you can admit that, you're on your way to maximizing your HR career, career path, and earning potential.

Let's dig into some steps we all need to take to heart related to the 9 Faces of HR, regardless of career level, industry, or location.

Step #1: Determine Which of The 9 Faces of HR You Are

To use the 9 Faces of HR to build your career, the first step is simple—take a behavioral assessment (with a cognitive component) to determine where you fall related to *cognitive ability/processing speed, assertiveness, rules orientation, and detail orientation.*

Behavioral assessments are a tool that most HR pros have used, are comfortable with, and have access to. While the behavioral dimensions listed above are called many different things by assessment companies (more of a preference/marketing decision), assertiveness, rules orientation, and detail orientation are generally included in some capacity in any behavioral assessment you purchase. Cognitive ability is not behavioral in nature, and as a result may or may not be included in your assessment package—you may have to seek out an assessment platform that includes it.

Once you've got your results, refer to the chapters detailing the 9 Faces of HR model. Determine your career level per the notes in Chapter 6, and then refer to the chapters detailing each of the 9 Faces of HR to compare your cognitive/behavioral profile (see the charts in each chapter) to find your match. Be sure to focus on the cognitive/behavioral components listed as "primary" for each of the 9 Faces, as those components are most important in finding your match.

After you've got your match, you're ready to use the 9 Faces of HR as a tool for your career development in HR.

Step #2: Understand Your Strength Is Also Your Weakness

For the record, let me first say I understand and appreciate management books and themes like *StrengthFinders*, which serve as calls to action to maximize strengths and deprioritize weaknesses (both in ourselves and the people we manage/provide guidance to). I embrace these concepts even though I'm more jaded than many HR pros I know.

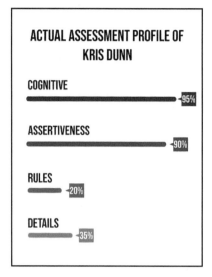

Figure 24.1. Scorecard for KD

Now for some real talk. *People get developed for their strengths and fired for their weaknesses.*

The people in HR who lose their jobs in the changing HR jobs marketplace are almost always eliminated with an eye towards perceived cognitive or behavioral weakness.

Here's where it gets tricky—your biggest strength can also be your biggest weakness. Need some examples?

High Cognitive

» **Strength:** Having more processing speed is almost always desired. The ability to take in large amounts of data and make quick, accurate decisions is valued in almost every job in today's world.
» **Potential Weakness:** High Cognitive people move fast, at times finish other people's sentences, and may be perceived as making decisions too rapidly without all the data needed, etc.

High Assertive

» **Strength:** Being willing to take action and confront people, teams, and situations that need to be addressed on some level is key to getting organizational results.

» **Potential Weakness:** Individuals with the highest assertiveness scores are often seen as overly aggressive. The resulting reputation of being poor team members and collaborators can hinder career success, especially in cultures with the charter of "no jerks."

High Rules

» **Strength:** If you want something done according to specifications, high rules people are valued for their ability to execute by the book.

» **Potential Weakness:** High rules team members can be stereotyped as low innovators with limited ability to think outside the box. They are also known to be low performers in chaotic environments with limited rules and are frustrated by high levels of change.

Low Rules

» **Strength:** If you must drop someone into a structureless environment, the low rules person is your choice. Not bothered by a corporate or organizational free-for-all with zero norms, this person will thrive in chaos.

» **Potential Weakness:** The low rules teammate hates structure. If you need them to follow the rules, it's not going to go well. Low rules workers commonly thrive in early stage companies and become liabilities as structure and bureaucracy creeps in.

High Details

» **Strength:** Being high details is a leading indicator of someone's ability to be organized and, as a result, execute.

> **Potential Weakness:** This persona will value details and organization over all else. High details team members are, at times, viewed as underperformers at thinking beyond the spreadsheet. They would rather check off something on their list than divert to a non-planned activity.

What's all this mean? You've got strengths, but you've also got weaknesses in your behavioral profile. The thing that may end up getting you in the end isn't your clearly identified weakness, but your super strength that is viewed as a liability by people who are wired differently than you are. Know your super strength and keep your head on a swivel for folks who matter growing sour on what makes you special.

Step #3: Know Who Is in Power and What They Think Great HR Looks Like

Now you have awareness of your super strengths as well as how they could be held against you in organizational gymnastics gone wild. Seems like the right time for a political lesson related to the 9 Faces of HR.

We talked earlier about organizational change, aka *"Your Future Boss Thinks You Suck."* Let's go a little bit deeper and analyze the kinds of players your new boss could be that you ultimately have to impress.

1. **The Change Agent.** If you report to the C-level and there's involuntary churn, odds are the new person is coming in with a "let's turbocharge this thing" type of vibe. That means every functional area, including HR, is subject to hard evaluation and the top grading that goes with it. The Change Agent generally wants to see big ideas and innovation coming from HR. If you're on the left of the 9 Faces of HR (Judge,

Cop), get ready to pivot a bit. We should note that not every Change Agent comes in with guns blazing towards HR. At times, Change Agents are brought in for adult leadership at high growth companies with a focus on installing structure and risk management. In those circumstances, HR leaders on the right of the 9 Faces of HR grid may feel some pressure. See the section in this book detailing change at Uber for an example of this change.

While Change Agents are the primary new boss persona that HR leaders will see at the C-level, I couldn't leave this chapter without providing tools to all the HR coordinators, managers, directors, and HRBPs that get a new CHRO or SVP of HR at the top of their company's food chain. Understanding which of the 9 Faces of HR the new boss of HR personifies is key to surviving and thriving moving forward.

2. **The Judge.** If you're the Cop or the Machine, you've got the same DNA as your new boss and should be thrilled. Look at the profile of the Judge elsewhere in this book and you'll find a highly assertive, high rules leader who's going to limit risk. If you're the Rookie or the Assassin, you might want to lay low for a little bit. Your desire to work on exciting new projects feels risky to the Judge. If you want to stick around, you might want to neutralize some of your low rules, renegade ways.

3. **The Mentor.** I've got good news and bad news. The good news is that the Mentor wants you to be successful in your career as a part of their new team. The bad news is that they expect results and won't do the work for you. There is a slight advantage here to the Assassin and the Rookie, who love project-based work. However, there is opportunity here for the Fixer and the Clerk to show what they're capable of. Heads up to the Cop and the

Machine to appear somewhat interested in undefined projects that may get pushed to your plate.

4. **The Natural.** You went to the meet and greet, and they seemed awesome. There's opportunity with the Natural in the CHRO chair for everyone to be themselves. The Cop and the Machine (as well as the Fixer and the Clerk) should reinforce what they're good at and make the Natural confident that all the messy stuff will be handled for them. The Assassin and the Rookie will be able to do what they're best at. Peace will be the vibe as long as you do your job because the Natural is chill as hell.

Step #4: Put Your Knowledge to Work by Looking/Sounding the Part

This is the easiest step related to using the 9 Faces of HR to build your career. Please do the following:

1. Understand who you are in the 9 Faces of HR.
2. Understand which persona you're dealing with at the C-level or HR leadership level (based on your role).
3. If your 9 Faces persona is aligned with what that person wants, **let your freak flag fly**.
4. If your 9 Faces persona is not aligned with that leadership FTE, turn the volume down on your preferred mode of working, which is to say, **do not let your freak flag fly**.

What goes into "not letting your freak flag fly?" That's just a fancy way of saying don't expose yourself as being the behavioral opposite of the person you're reporting to. More important to this self-awareness is actually providing some work, performance, and commentary that is aligned with your new boss's world view. Examples include:

» You're High Rules and fall to the left of the 9 Faces of HR grid. To neutralize being viewed as low innovation, you volunteer to lead a couple of projects from scratch for The Mentor or The Natural, then you work your ass off to create value. The unstructured work absolutely drains your life batteries to zero, but you've bought yourself one to two years of cover with the new boss by making this calculated investment. Well played.

» You're Low Rules and fall to the right of the 9 Faces of HR grid. To ensure you don't fall out of favor in your first quarter with a CHRO who is a Judge, you roll out a project that's all about brutal compliance as the first thing you want to chase under her tutelage. The project feels like a death march, and you now know more about Fair Labor Standards Act (FLSA) than most lawyers. You bought yourself at least a year, and some grace, from the Judge when you blow something up, which will happen. It always does.

You call it sucking up. The board of viability for your career (I'm the chairman) calls it smart as hell. Become self-aware, use the 9 Faces as your guide, and play the game.

Step #5: Find a Place You Can Be Yourself

Our last step related to using the 9 Faces of HR to build your career is to be a smarter shopper.

I hope you're at your company for the rest of your career. For most of us, that's not going to happen. When HR pros get unhappy, we usually shop for their next opportunity. Now that you understand who you are in the 9 Faces of HR, you've got an opportunity to become a savvier, smarter candidate. When it comes to what career opportunity provides the best fit for you, there are four factors you need to evaluate.

1. Self. This whole book is about you as an HR pro. See the rest of the book and have self-awareness of who you are and what makes you tick.

2. The company/HR structure/job. It stands to reason that the company you're thinking about joining drives a lot of your future satisfaction and career success. But instead of focusing on what the company does and how successful it is (all good things to evaluate), I want you to focus on the type of work HR does in that organization and how the job you're thinking about taking delivers value. If you fall to the left of the 9 Faces of HR, you should be looking for a company with strong HR infrastructure and a HR role that's about supporting that infrastructure with precision. If you fall to the right of the 9 Faces of HR, you should be looking for a company and a role with less structure, a place where you'll have a chance to create. HR pros in the middle of the 9 Faces of HR can thrive in both environments. Regardless of your HR face, you can find happiness at any size company. It's more about knowing how HR works at that company and the specific requirements of the role you'll be going into.

3. The potential boss. Know who your boss is behaviorally. It's okay to not match them, but you need some directionally accurate information that suggests they'll value your DNA and want you to contribute on those terms. The best HR organizations will make an assessment as part of their process, openly share your results, and talk candidly about what they see and your resulting fit.

4. The team. You'll always be considering new opportunities with less than perfect data, but it's great to know a bit about the team you'll be joining. While you may be focused on confirming the team is pleasant and nice, I'd suggest it's

probably more important that your face in the 9 Faces of HR is a complement to what already exists on the team and that you'll be valued as a result.

HR pros are great at providing career counsel to others, but sometimes we forget to take care of ourselves. Figure out which one of the 9 Faces of HR you are, and be selfish when it comes to your maximizing career by leveraging the knowledge and self-awareness.

25

Build It and They Will Come: Using the 9 Faces of HR as a CHRO/VP of HR

Gettin' good players is easy.
Gettin' 'em to play together is the hard part.
—Casey Stengel

If you're an HR leader reading this book, you have the most important job—building an HR team to satisfy the growing needs of the business leaders you support as you swim in a sea of stereotypes about our profession. As Run-DMC once said, "it's tricky." You need to build a team capable of handling the transactional side of your business while creating a capacity to innovate, drive change, and add value. With every selection you make for your team, you're placing a bet on future delivery.

Balance and Capacity should be your mantra as you build your team.

Of course, for all the capability you have as an HR Leader, you're still hopelessly human. You've got your own likes and dislikes, your own biases, and it's only reasonable to assume those will impact the choices you make.

That's why we've put the following guide together for how to use the 9 Faces of HR as a CHRO or VP of HR (or whatever your HR leadership title is). Follow the steps we've outlined on the pages that follow to build an HR team that's balanced and has the capacity to deliver in a constantly evolving business environment.

Step #1: Figure Out Who You Are

Great HR leadership first requires incredible self-awareness. You've already got that to a large degree, or you wouldn't be in the role you're in. Time to take the next step. Take a behavioral assessment with a cognitive component to determine where you fall in cognitive ability/processing speed, assertiveness, rules orientation, and detail orientation.

Once you've got your results, refer to the earlier chapters detailing Judge, the Mentor, and the Natural. Normalize your scores from the four areas into percentages (think of a bell curve), compare your cognitive/behavioral profile to the charts in each chapter, and find your match.

Got a read related to which one of the leadership personas you are? Great! Now do the following to really let it sink in.

» **Feel the burn and think about what your profile means.** If you were completely honest with yourself, most of you aren't the Natural. That's okay because even though it's a really cool title, I'm not sure that's the best HR leader for most companies. If your DNA points to you being a Judge, that's going to bum some of you out a little bit. Don't despair. You've got some command and control in your DNA, and it's likely how you rose to the top. Understand who you are and look for more opportunities to lead initiatives that are innovative and drive change. You're capable of that, or you wouldn't be in the role. If you're a Mentor, you're probably proud and relieved because that title feels better than the Judge. Don't celebrate too much, because you've got things to work on. Your reliance on helping other people grow can lead to efficiency blind spots, and if we know anything about HR, it's that the details can kill you. We've all got things to celebrate and work on.

» **Identify gaps as well as areas that might be unusual strengths.** Read up on the feature chapters in this book profiling the Judge, the Mentor, and the Natural. Everyone's cognitive and behavioral DNA is a little bit different. The gaps related to how these profiles interact with the world are detailed in those chapters, but you may have some traits that make you special in the secondary characteristics of each profile.

Examples—You may be a Judge with a very high cognitive score in addition to the high rules/high assertiveness anchors, which means transitioning to thinking about innovation and change will be easier for you than some of your peers. Or you may be a Mentor with an extremely high details score, signaling you'll thrive in huge corporate initiatives like ramping up a shared service center or a complete overhaul of recruiting.

» **Control the "like me" bias.** No section on figuring out who you are for an HR leader would be complete without this reminder. You are who you are. We all love people who are like us, and that's dangerous for any HR leader in control. Start getting comfortable and reminding yourself of the need to hire people who are different than you by using the 9 Faces of HR model.

You've built a career on being more aware than most. The 9 Faces of HR will help you take that to the next level.

Step #2: Figure Out Who You Have

Once you understand who you are across the 9 Faces of HR, you need to take inventory of what you've got across the entire HR team. Put together a project plan heavy on communication and knock out these projects.

1. **Put everyone through an assessment with a cognitive component.** Follow the instructions provided for you in the figure out who you are step of this chapter. Find an assessment to map out the four factors in the 9 Faces of HR model.

Give the assessment to everyone from the lowest level HR assistant to your direct reports.

2. **Map it all out. Celebrate strengths and show the map to the team.** Once you get the results back, transparency is key. Share the profiles with individuals and take the next step and map out where all team members fall on the four factors included in the 9 Faces of HR model. The smartest HR leaders will follow this project plan to meet everyone's needs and sensitivities:

    »   Hold individual meetings first to cover the assessment results one-on-one.

    »   Once those one-on-ones are complete, set up a time to meet as a team to cover how the team looks across the assessment categories. Don't distribute the team map before you meet. Cover the team results in that session and then provide the team map as a leave behind resource for everyone on the team. You don't have to identify the face that each specific HR team member is. The strength is in the awareness per category.

3. **Install a coaching model designed to emphasize strengths and neutralize weakness.** It's good to assess and be transparent about the results across the team. To take it to the next level, we recommend installing a coaching model where the assessment results are used to emphasize strengths and neutralize weaknesses. This model can be as simple as identifying each HR team member's top two strengths and top two areas for growth (remember that one category could actually be both depending on context and circumstances) in an initial coaching session. The manager for each individual would continue to focus on the 2×2 model in one-on-ones, performance check ins, etc.

Skipping this step as an HR leader is bad. If you don't take the time to build the map of your team, all subsequent steps are guesswork.

Step #3: Determine Who You Really Need

Here's where the 9 Faces of HR gets fun. If you do the work and understand who you are as an HR leader and where the rest of the team falls, you can be strategic about understanding your needs and planning for the future. Do the following related to strategic planning using the 9 Faces of HR:

1. **Do a gap analysis across the 9 Faces of HR.** You mapped your HR team using assessment categories in step two, but you likely stopped short of telling them they were a Cop, Assassin, or Fixer. That's okay—I get it. Now's the time for you to plot the team on the actual 9 Faces of HR grid. Using career level and the cognitive and behavioral charts in each chapter, map out the team accordingly.

   See the gaps? Make notes about what is abundant on your team and what's missing. Some of you may have teams stacked with Cops and Machines, while others may have heavy Fixer and Clerk representation. Few of you will be loaded with Assassins and Rookies for historical reasons discussed previously in this book.

2. **Make sure you have at least one renegade at all times.** Speaking of Assassins and Rookies, note that if you don't have a member of your HR team on the far right of the grid, that should be your first recruiting priority. This is your first priority because your function needs diversity related to how the collective team views innovation, change, and adding value that business partners see as meaningful.

3. **Get comfortable with lower level HR pros being sources of innovation if your mid-level incumbents are high rules.** Many of you will have mid-level direct reports who are high rules and, as a result, if you have team members to the right of the grid, they'll fit the profile of the Rookie. This is better than having no team members in this area, so you'll just need to provide more coaching and guidance as they chase innovation and value-added activities. You'll need to harness the ambition with daily contact to ensure change.

Mapping your team on the 9 Faces of HR grid is key to being honest about your team's capabilities.

Step #4: Recruit Accordingly

Say it with me: *Every opening on your HR team is an opportunity to build balance and capacity.* You don't always control what job is open, but you do control who you hire. When a replacement or new budgeted position is available and ready to be posted, go back to the team map you created related to the 9 Faces of HR. What do you need more of? Regardless of career level (early or mid-career), your goal should be to build more balance related to your team's ability to innovate, drive change, and add value.

For most, this will mean seeking out more talent to the right of the 9 Faces of HR model. Job postings and job descriptions matter in this process. Whether you're trying to attract a Rookie or an Assassin, these marketing tools should reflect what you want them to accomplish in the role. The same concept holds true if you're looking for mid-range or low ability to innovate. Write postings designed to attract the candidate you want. Don't use standard, bland language.

There are other important things to remember when recruiting for specific personas. It should go without saying, but don't guess on the cognitive and behavioral DNA of your candidates. Use the same assessment you used with your team and use the tool on all of your finalists.

Consider an assessment profile in your selection process with the proper weight. If your direct report is doing the hiring, be sure the mandate is clear on the profile you're looking to hire. We all suffer from the "like me" bias, and your direct reports aren't immune to this phenomenon. You'll probably need to see the assessment profile and do a short interview to check-off on-hires.

Do all of these things, and you'll be on track to build the right type of balance and capacity.

A Special Note to My "HR Department of One" Friends

I see you. You're the HR leader for a small company with an HR team ranging from one to four people (including you), and you've got the rare, but important, opportunity to hire for your HR team. You can't possibly have all the bases covered related to the 9 Faces of HR. What do you do?

For most of you, the biggest question you have to answer is: do you dare hire the Rookie for your HR support role? It's an important question because you'd love to get someone with the ability to innovate and drive change mixed in with transactional duties out of the FTE in question. Many of you will conduct your process, and if you use an assessment per my earlier recommendation, you'll have a Rookie in your recruiting mix.

The answer is pretty simple. You hire a Rookie for your transactional role only if you can stomach being a training ground for new college grads for one to two years before they move to another company (usually for more money and a better title). I'm a believer in this path because the right hire in this role can help you elevate the HR function at your company.

If you can't stomach the turnover, you should hire the Machine or the Clerk as part of your 9 Faces of HR recruiting process.

Build It and They Will Come

You've got the most important job in the world—building an HR team the business leaders you support will love and respect. Build your team with a focus on balance, capacity, and an eye toward being able to innovate, and you'll not only have a high performing HR function, but be a destination of choice for the HR pros you most want to recruit.

26

C-Level Notes: Using The 9 Faces of HR Model to Find and Select a CHRO/VP of HR

*It's very easy to find a new one, but
it's hard to find a true one.*
—Unknown

It's clear based on our experience that the 9 Faces of HR provides a smart backdrop for HR pros at all levels to understand who they are, the signals they send, and how to prepare for the evolving future world of HR. It's also clear that our model provides a great search methodology for companies seeking to find the transformative HR talent they need to drive business results.

This chapter is for companies embarking on searches for their next great HR pro, usually at the senior leadership level. Since our model was built through retained and contingency HR searches at Kinetix, we have an informed opinion about how to best use the 9 Faces of HR to determine the fit and utility of candidates being considered in your search.

Simply put, the 9 Faces of HR eliminates much of the guesswork and variability you face in any HR search. The following represents our view of the most important aspects of using our model as you seek the best candidate for your open HR leadership role.

Most Companies Want the Natural or an Assassin, but...

As you consider using the 9 Faces of HR in your next HR leadership search, let's knock out an important barrier to your success. You're going to read the chapters in this book, download the model in your mind, and then make the following determination.

You're going to decide you need the Natural or an Assassin for your open HR spot.

Odds are you'll be wrong. While we love both personas in our model and across the world of HR, hiring the Natural or the Assassin can be problematic. Our body of work using the model suggests that the Natural represents well under one percent of the total HR workforce. You'll be hard pressed to find the Natural and when you do, retention is always an issue (see our chapter on the Natural for more information on this issue).

The Assassin is no less problematic. If it's change you seek for HR inside your company, the Assassin seems like a logical choice. But your eyes may be bigger than your stomach in this regard. Hiring an Assassin comes with the requirement that they'll be allowed to do what they do best—work in a low-rule, fast, assertive style—and be supported when they blow things up and feelings inside the company and HR team are hurt as a result. Many companies want what the Assassin does best but struggle to support them once they're in the door.

The Right Intake Process Is Key— Where Do You Want to Go?

The easy solution is to always have a strong intake meeting designed to outline everything you want and need your future HR leader to be, but to also evaluate the environment the HR leader will be plugged into. While most traditional intakes focus on job responsibilities and compensation, getting the right fit using the 9 Faces of HR model adds the following components.

» **What are the biggest issues and projects you expect the HR leader to tackle in their first year?** Understanding your goals is an important step in any intake process for an HR leader. If you simply seek to keep things moving consistent with the status quo, you don't need to move to the far right in the 9 Faces grid.

» **Does your business place a premium on raw execution or is it knowledge intensive?** HR leaders like the Judge are usually best placed in established companies delivering products and services through mature processes. Business models heavy with intellectual capital are best served by the Mentor, and in somewhat rare circumstances, the Natural.

» **What's the history of HR at your company? What do you want to change?** Reputation of the HR function may be neutral at best, which means many organizations seek to elevate HR via the opportunity to hire a new HR leader. This is a noble goal, but to really understand the need, you have to dig into the history of HR at your company. What's been missing, lost opportunities, HR metrics, etc. are all items that should be assessed when determining the best 9 Faces leadership profile for your team.

» **Who are you as a leader?** What do you want most from your relationship with the HR Leader you'll hire? Your style as a leader impacts the success of the search more than you think. Do you allow your leadership team direct reports to fail? Are you a command and control leader? Who you are strongly impacts the right hire and the 9 Faces persona that's the best fit for you.

» **What does your leadership team want most from HR?** Will they be supportive of change in this area? In many companies, the HR leader has a history of being a second-class citizen when it comes to having influence on the leadership team. In most cases, this is due to the performance and caliber of the previous HR leader before you opened the search. You'll need to set the stage for the next HR leader you land via this search through strong onboarding and setting expectations with your leadership team.

Answering all of these questions via a strong intake process creates the successful profile for your HR leadership search. Once the intake is complete, using the 9 Faces of HR guides the recruiting process by focusing your efforts on one of the three leadership profiles contained in the model—the Natural, the Mentor, or the Judge.

Know Your Existing HR Staff

When you embark on any HR leadership search, it's a good idea to look at the HR team your selected candidate will lead. Simply put, the aggregate profile of the HR team you have in place also influences the right type of candidate for your search.

If you have a highly transactional HR team, hiring a Judge is easy if you want to maintain status quo moving forward. If you're looking to transform your HR function, you'll need a Mentor, but be aware—the transformation you seek is likely going to result in some attrition on the HR team, both voluntary and involuntary.

Inverse considerations hold true as well. If your HR team includes profiles like the Fixer and the Clerk, as well as more innovative ones like the Assassin and the Rookie, you'll need to hire a Mentor to make it work. Hiring the Judge will likely cause intermediate term attrition of the Rookie and Assassin profiles, and it likely won't be the type of attrition you desire.

The 9 Faces of HR Might Be About
Three Hires Instead of One

Many of you reading this and thinking about an HR leadership hire are seeking true transformation. Being realistic about what's required in any HR transformation is key. It's likely that hiring an HR leader won't be enough. You'll need to make multiple hires to give your HR leader the talent they need to be successful.

A Note to CHRO/VP of HR Types
Conducting Mid-Level HR Searches

While this chapter has focused on providing notes on the use of the 9 Faces of HR for C-level executives and board of directors conducting HR leadership searches, the same principles hold true for CHROs and VPs of HR conducting mid-level searches. Use the resources outlined in this book and the intake process questions in this chapter (modified for your span of control) for optimal results in finding the best HR director, manager, and HRBP candidates to meet your needs. Fit matters. The 9 Faces of HR provides a comprehensive model to guide your next HR search.

27
Career Mobility Inside The 9 Faces of HR Model

She should go far. The sooner she starts, the better.
—Anonymous

No tour of the 9 Faces of HR model would be complete without the consideration of career mobility and career pathing. After all, if you're going to buy into the 9 Faces of HR model as you build your future-proof HR function, you'll need to know what you can count on from a succession planning perspective.

The easy answer is that senior level HR pros have climbed the career mountain and are well-placed and each of the columns in the model provides natural succession planning (low/middle/high ability to innovate, drive change, and add value as you look at the columns left to right across the 9 Faces of HR).

Before we provide commentary on the career paths for each of the early career and mid-career personas in our model, here's our

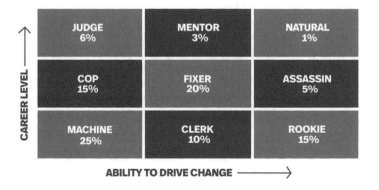

Figure 27.1. Career Mobility

estimate of how the HR world breaks down by percentage across the 9 Faces of HR.

Estimates provided are reflective of our experience in the world of HR search and actual candidates applying for open searches used in research to develop the 9 Faces of HR model. Our work estimates that the entire world of HR is made up of 50 percent early career, 40 percent mid-career, and 10 percent senior-level HR pros.

Note that these percentages may vary based on your definition of each level. Consider a sample of ten HR professionals in the field, and five of ten being entry-level sounds reasonable. Your experience with HR might move the percentages lower starting from the top (less than 10 percent senior level, less than 40 percent mid-career), but they certainly would not move the percentages higher if you accurately assess true level that transcends title. Company size, years of experience, and other factors must be measured to truly assess level.

The Fixer Is the Pivot Position in HR Succession

While it is correct to say each of the columns in the model provides natural succession planning—low/middle/high ability to innovate, drive change, and add value as you look at the columns left to right across the 9 Faces of HR—there's one position in the model that deserves special consideration.

The Fixer may be the most important position to consider in HR succession planning. Let's flash back to our early profile of this persona to understand why.

The Fixer has a DNA profile that's decidedly unspectacular but well suited for their role. Since Fixers are mid-career HR pros at the manager, director, and HRBP levels with employee client groups, the preferred DNA profile is one of balance.

The consideration for HR succession is obvious. While the Cop is also responsible for client groups in most HR organizations, their lack of balance (extreme rules and details scores) leads to average outcomes when compared to the Fixer. See the earlier chapters on both the Fixer and the Cop for a deeper dive on how they are different.

Because every HR candidate and employee has cognitive and behavioral scores that exist on a continuum and are not absolute, employees designated as the Machine or the Rookie may have a career path to the Fixer position in the 9 Faces of HR. Key to this potential would be moderation in a single primary cognitive and behavioral characteristic primary to their persona.

For example, the Machine is high rules and high details. If rules orientation exists at the 70th percentile, instead of the 90th percentile, they have a career path into the Fixer role as well as the Cop. It likely depends on the coaching, mentoring, and career development they receive. Similarly, a Rookie with a moderate instead of an extreme low rules score (think 35th percentile instead of 10th) can flow into the Fixer role instead of the Assassin role.

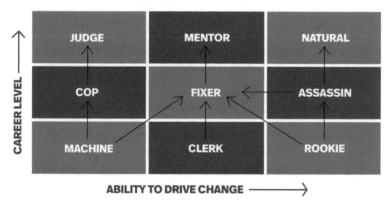

Figure 27.2. Career Path

Deeper Notes on Career Paths for Early and Mid-Career HR Pros

Here's a chart showing directional career paths for the 9 Faces of HR. Take a look and we'll discuss all of the early to mid-career HR roles after the jump.

Here are some quick hitting notes about each career path:

» **The Machine:** The natural career path for this high rules, high detail individual is to the Cop role, where they'll pick up client responsibilities and continue to rule via command and control. A secondary career path flows to the Fixer role if their high rules score is moderate, as described in the previous section.

» **The Clerk:** This balanced early career HR pro has a single career path to the Fixer role.

» **The Rookie:** This high cog, low rules, high details individual has a natural career path to the Assassin role, where their ambition and need to drive change can be fed. If the Rookie has a moderately low rules score, rather than an extreme low rules score, they can ascend to the Fixer role. In addition, HR leaders often move Rookies into HR manager roles with client group responsibilities (a feature of the Fixer role) to shut them up by showing them how hard the real world and employee relations can be.

» **The Cop:** This hard core, high rules/high details manager has one path for a next step. They're either going to become the Judge or stay where they are. Cops with high assertiveness scores in addition to the rules/details markers become Judges, and those without high assertiveness in their DNA stay mid-level for the rest of their careers.

» **The Fixer:** If this balanced HR pro has both cognitive and assertiveness scores that tick up from the mean towards the 70th-75th percentile, they are promotable over time to the Mentor role. If they don't possess this profile tweak, they're presumed to be well-placed at the mid-level role.

» **The Assassin:** It's a hard knock life for the Assassin from a succession perspective. The Assassin makes enemies inside any organization in a short period of time. If coached and mentored aggressively, the candidate can ascend to the senior level. Extreme Assassins (very low rules, very high assertiveness) rarely make it to the top, but those with moderately low rules or high assertiveness scores have a chance.

Don't Forget to Assess Your Needs Before You Promote

Before you promote any of the six personas explored here from a succession perspective, be sure to understand your organizational needs. Needs and results vary by circumstance. The 9 Faces of HR is an effective tool to guide you, but you know your business best. Proceed with succession planning promotions with due diligence and care.

28
Closing Time

You don't have to go home, but you can't stay here.
—Semisonic

Are you buying what I'm selling? Is the world of HR and the resulting expectations of our function changing? Do you think you're going to wake up one day with a new boss, new circumstances in the world of HR, and be expected to do something different?

No? Then by all means, you should take the blue pill. You go back to your email, the story ends, you wake up in your bed tomorrow, and believe whatever you want to believe. For some of you, that will work out fine. For others, it ends with change-based pain.

But if you believe some, or all, of the core concepts I've covered in this book (HR has an innovation problem, HR stereotypes are killing our profession, and top jobs—at the C-level and in HR leadership—are increasingly going to leaders who want different things from HR pros) *you're likely to take the red pill.*

I worked on The 9 Faces of HR model and wrote this book because I believe that great HR has an undeniable impact on every business in which it is embedded—all the way to impacting revenue and profitability. When you take the red pill related to The 9 Faces of HR, you're acknowledging that change is happening rapidly around you in the world of HR, and you might have to adjust the way you think to maximize your influence, as well as your career.

You don't have to change who you are. You just need to maximize your awareness and agility. The best advice I can give you is to follow the five-step plan in Chapter 24, which goes like this:

Step #1—Determine which of the 9 Faces of HR you are

Step #2—Understand your strength is also your weakness

Step #3—Know who is in power and what they think great HR looks like

Step #4—Put that knowledge to work by looking and sounding the part

Step #5—Find a place you can be yourself

That chapter is the roadmap for putting The 9 Faces of HR to work in your career. Implied in that game plan is the fact that you need to do great work, deliver more than is expected, and generally kick a lot of a** as an HR pro. Being politically savvy, once you understand your strengths and weaknesses within The 9 Faces of HR model, is only half of the equation—great work completes the circle and makes you essential/critical to those who matter.

I hope you take the time to consider who you are and how you fit into the 9 Faces of HR. There's no such thing as a good face or a bad face in this model—low self-awareness is the only attribute we should consider lame.

I love HR pros who want to surprise people by bucking the stereotypes. Go create something this month at your company that delights five people—and pisses at least one person off.

Index

Symbols

9-box grid 49–50, 55–62, 107

A

A.I. (artificial intelligence) 26, 209–10

Amazon 122

analysts 75

Angelou, Maya 181

Annenberg University 40

annual merit increase 31, 62

Apple 35, 99

applicant tracking system (ATS) 149

Archer 10

artificial intelligence (A.I.) 26, 209–10

assertiveness 66, 79

assessment platforms 101

The Atlantic 44–45

ATS (applicant tracking system) 149

AT&T 41

Atwood, Renee 143

automation 203, 208

awareness 221

B

Baauer 34

balance, work/life 169, 217

Banks, Jonathan 164

becoming mass-market 33

behavioral factors 65

behavior, passive 17

benefits 170

Benioff, Marc 44

big, hairy, audacious goal (BHAG) 96
  categories of 96–97

Billboard 34

Blazing Saddles 89

Bleed American 193

Bock, Lazlo 71

bootstrapper 6

Born This Way 65

bosses
  managing new 217–20
  types of 225

branding, culture 43

Breaking Bad 164

Bridesmaids 49

Broderick, Matthew 221

Brown, Mary Beth 95

building culture 140

Business Insider 143

C

capital
  human 5
  human sector 182
  intellectual 140, 241

capologist, HR 75

career
  building, steps for 222–29
  development 247
  level 50–51, 108, 279–80
  mobility and pathing 198, 245
  path 5
  paths, directional 247–49

cash cow 188

certification 190

change and HR 38–40, 213–19

Cheadle, Don 55

chief equality officer 46

chief human resource officer
(CHRO) 121, 143, 182, 189, 193

chief people officer 111

Chiklis, Michael 173

CHRO (chief human resource officer).
See chief human resource officer
(CHRO)

Citicorp 97

Clarkson, Patricia 164

CNBC 210

coaching 31, 186, 247
model 234

cognitive
ability 66, 71
assessment 72
component 71–74
skills 69

compensation equity 44

confrontation 18

consulting 139

co-opting 35

corporate
ladder 121
paratrooper 7

corporate social responsibility
(CSR) 43

Cruise, Tom 121

CSR (corporate social
responsibility) 43

culture 145
branding 43
building 140

D

Davidson College 194

Deadpool 79

detail orientation 66, 101–6

development, software 2

The Devil Wears Prada 213

Dictionary.com 80

Dirty Harry 5

diversity 45–47, 105

diversity hiring 44

Drake 33

Dunn, Kris (KD) 8, 21

E

Eastwood, Clint 5

The Economist 210

Ellington, Duke 37

*Elon Musk: Tesla, SpaceX, and the Quest
for a Fantastic Future* 95

emerging trends 38–42

employee relations 85–87

employer value proposition (EVP) 99

The Enforcer 10

equality 45–47

EVP (employer value proposition) 99

expectations of managers 30

*Expert Political Judgment: How Good Is
It? How Can We Know?* 40

F

factors, behavioral 65–67

Fair Labor Standards Act (FLSA) 228

falling into HR 6–8

Ferris Bueller's Day Off 221

financial services 139

firms, venture capital 133

Fistful of Talent 52, 189

The Five Dysfunctions of the Team 15

five-factor model 65

FLSA (Fair Labor Standards Act) 228

forecasting 40

framing 44

full-time employee (FTE) 75

FX 10

G

gamification 288

Gates, Bill 38–40

gaydar 209–12

gender pay gap 44

GitHub 26

Glip 202

God's Plan 34

Google 71

Graham, Kent 101

growth opportunities 140

The Guardian 97

H

Handelsbatt 99

Harlem Shake 34

headhunter 112

healthcare 139

high potential employee (HIPO) 7, 115

hiring
  diversity 44
  managers 158

hiring manager batting average (HMBA) 158

Holder, Eric 146

hooks for mass-market 35

Hornsey, Liane 143–47

Hotline Bling 35

House of Cards 164

House of Lies 55

HR
  competencies for 92–93
  falling into 6–8
  functions 6–7, 37
  Hollywood and 10
  metrics and analytics 75–78
  stereotypes in 26, 37
  team profiles 242
  transformation of 242
  world percentages of 246

HR business resource partner (HRBP) 92, 206

The HR Capitalist 52, 189

HR haters
  behaviors of 16
  dealing with 18–19
  types of 14–15

HR leader
  behavioral dimensions 66
  challenges facing 58
  effectiveness of 77–78
  saying yes as 28–30

HRMS (human resource management system) 203

HR pro. See HR leader

human capital 44

human resource management system (HRMS) 203

I

Iacocca, Lee 69

IBM Global 9

industry
  attractiveness of 56
  competitive strength within 56

innovation 37–42, 93, 235–36

intake process 240

International Astronautical Congress 98

J

Jerry McGuire 121

Jimmy Eat World 193

Jobs, Steve 149

Journal of Personality and Social Psychology 210

K

Keitel, Harvey 164
Kemper, Ellie 49
Kinetix 52, 101, 239

L

Lady Gaga 65
leadership team (LT) 2, 122
learning ability 71–73
leave of absence (LOA) 202, 212
letter of authorization (LOA) 168
Life Starts Now 1
LinkedIn 9, 50, 144
LOA (leave of absence) 202, 212
LOA (letter of authorization) 168
Look What You Made Me Do 34
LT (leadership team) 2, 122

M

managers
   expectations of 30
   hiring 158
   managing new 217–20
manufacturing 139
Marilyn Brooks 9
marketing 43, 117
   opportunities 43
marketplace of ideas 43
mass-market hooks 35
master's in business administration (MBA) 8, 191
The Matrix 201
McCaw Cellular 41
McKinsey and Company 41, 56
mentoring 7, 247
Merck 97

merit increase, annual 31, 62
Microsoft 38
The Middle 193
models
   coaching 234
   five-factor 65
Moneyball 76
Musk, Elon 95, 97–99

N

negotiation tactics 18–19
New York Times 146
Nielsen Music 34
Nike 97
Northeast Missouri State 8

O

OD (organizational development) 76
The Office 10
Office Christmas Party 10
onboarding 193, 241
organizational safety 176
organization development (OD) 76

P

pay
   equity 44–47
   gap, gender-based 44
   for performance 170
people person 6
PE (private equity) 111
performance
   management 42, 57–63
   review 30
performance improvement plan (PIP) 174
performance vs. potential (PvP) 60–62
PIP (performance improvement plan) 174
Pitt, Brad 76

portfolio 192

predicting the future of HR 40

private equity (PE) 111

processing speed 66, 69, 75

product development 2

project work 219

promotability 192

Prophet, Tony 46

PR (public relations) 43

Psychology Today 80–81

public relations (PR) 43

Pulp Fiction 164

PvP (performance vs. potential) 60–62

Q

quantitative analyst 75

R

Ray Donovan 164

recruiters, contingency 2

recruiting 2, 7, 34–36, 238, 242
    marketing for 43

request for proposal (RFP) 9

resume sorter 190

retention 156, 240

return on investment (ROI) 5

revenue 78

revenue per employee (RPE) 76–78

Reynolds, Ryan 79

RFP (Request for Proposal) 9

ROI (return on investment) 5

rotational program 115

RPE (revenue per employee) 76–78

rules orientation 66, 89, 95, 102, 105

S

safety, organizational 176

salary cap in HR 76

Salesforce 43–47

Scandal 161, 164

Schreiber, Liev 164

search methodology 239

Semisonic 251

SEO (search engine optimization) 40

service organization 81

services, financial 139

Sheindlin, Judith 133

The Shield 173

SHRM Body of Knowledge 27, 37

SHRM (Society for Human Resources
    Management). *See Society for
    Human Resources Management
    (SHRM)*

Silicon Valley 44

SME (subject matter expert) 61

Society for Human Resources
    Management (SHRM) 5, 27, 189
    annual conference of 169

software development 2

Sony 97

SpaceX 95

Spotify 35

The Stanford University study 210

status quo 41, 215, 241, 242

Stengel, Casey 231

stereotypes in HR 26, 37

Streep, Meryl 213

StrengthFinders 222

subject matter expert (SME) 61

succession
    planning 245–49
    strategies 7

Swift, Taylor 25, 34

T

teammate
    high assertive 82

teammate (continued)
   high cognitive 73–74
   high details 103
   high rules 91–92
   low assertive 81
   low cognitive 72–73
   low details 102–3
   low rules 90–91

TechCrunch 46

Tesla 95

Tetlock, Phillip 40
   Tetlock Study 40

Three Days Grace 1

training 31
   ground 237

transformative HR 239

transformative PR 43

trends, emerging 38–42

Truman State 8

turnover 141, 157

types of boss 225

U

UAB (University of
   Alabama–Birmingham) 8

Uber 143–47

UBI (universal basic income) 203

UNC–Charlotte 194

Universal Basic Income (UBI) 203

University of Alabama–Birmingham
   (UAB) 8

Up in The Air 11

V

value-added work 192

Vance, Ashlee 95

venture capital firms 133

W

Wall Street Journal 85

WAR (wins above replacement) 76

Washington, Kerry 161, 164

Weaving, Hugo 201

Welch, Jack 169

West, Kanye 111

Winfrey, Oprah 121

wins above replacement (WAR) 76

work
   value-added 192
   worldview 95, 140, 192

About the Author

Who is Kris Dunn? That's an easy question. He's a VP of HR type who has led HR practices in *Fortune* 500s and venture capital-held startups. He works for a living, and believes that the key to great business results is to get great people, then do cool stuff to maximize their motivation, performance, and effectiveness once you have them in the door. As it turns out, that's his simple definition of talent management. He believes that all forms of HR and recruiting administration should be squeezed down to the smallest amount of time possible, giving you more time to do stuff that matters.

If you like that description, then you'll like Kris. It's that simple. If you need a more professional rundown, here are his stats: three degrees. One marriage. An SPHR that's been recertified twice. 5,000+ hires. 1,000+ fires. A taste for grunge music originating from Seattle. Two turntables. One microphone.

Kris is also among the most transparent HR pros you can find, and here's why. He cares so much about the art of HR and recruiting that he's started two blogs with the goal of building communities he could learn from. He's been writing his thoughts down every business day for ten years. Recently recognized as one of *Human Resource Executive* Top HR Tech Influencers, Kris has written nearly 100 columns for *Workforce Management* magazine, and has keynoted more than 100 conferences and events.

That means what you see is what you get. Kris can't hide, and if he ever pulled the blogs down, Google would probably haunt him forever anyway.

Kris is currently the chief human resources officer for Kinetix, a national RPO/recruiting firm based in Atlanta, and the founder/editor-in-chief of *The HR Capitalist* and *Fistful of Talent*.

When he's not working, Kris can be found on a basketball court providing his sons with immediate feedback as they attempt to reach 10,000 hours of deliberate practice, as celebrated in Malcolm Gladwell's *Outliers*.

Other SHRM Books

A Manager's Guide to Developing Competencies in HR Staff
Tips and Tools for Improving Proficiency in Your Reports
Phyllis G. Hartman, SHRM-SCP

Actualized Leadership
Meeting Your Shadow and Maximizing Your Potential
William L. Sparks

California Employment Law: A Guide for Employers
Revised and Updated 2018 Edition
James J. McDonald, Jr., JD

Digital HR
A Guide to Technology-Enabled HR
Deborah Waddill, Ed.D.

Extinguish Burnout
A Practical Guide to Prevention and Recovery
Robert Bogue and Terri Bogue

From Hello to Goodbye: Second Edition
Proactive Tips for Maintaining Positive Employee Relations
Christine V. Walters, JD, SHRM-SCP

From We Will to At Will
A Handbook for Veteran Hiring, Transitioning, and Thriving in the Workplace
Justin Constantine with Andrew Morton

Go Beyond the Job Description
A 100-Day Action Plan for Optimizing Talents and Building Engagement
Ashley Prisant Lesko, Ph.D., SHRM-SCP

The HR Career Guide
Great Answers to Tough Career Questions
Martin Yate, CPC

HR on Purpose!!
Developing Deliberate People Passion
Steve Browne, SHRM-SCP

Investing in People
Financial Impact of Human Resource Initiatives, 3rd edition
Wayne F. Cascio, John W. Boudreau, and Alexis A. Fink

Mastering Consultation as an HR Practitioner
Making an Impact on Small Businesses
Jennifer Currence, SHRM-SCP

Motivation-Based Interviewing
A Revolutionary Approach to Hiring the Best
Carol Quinn

The Practical Guide to HR Analytics
Using Data to Inform, Transform, and Empower HR Decisions
Shonna D. Waters, Valerie N. Streets, Lindsay A. McFarlane, and Rachel Johnson-Murray

The Power of Stay Interviews for Engagement and Retention
Second Edition
Richard P. Finnegan

Predicting Business Success
Using Smarter Analytics to Drive Results
Scott Mondore, Hannah Spell, Matt Betts, and Shane Douthitt

The Recruiter's Handbook
A Complete Guide for Sourcing, Selecting, and Engaging the Best Talent
Sharlyn Lauby, SHRM-SCP

The SHRM Essential Guide to Employment Law
A Handbook for HR Professionals, Managers, and Businesses
Charles H. Fleischer, JD

Solve Employee Problems Before They Start
Resolving Conflict in the Real World
Scott Warrick

The Talent Fix
A Leader's Guide to Recruiting Great Talent
Tim Sackett, SHRM-SCP

Books Approved for SHRM Recertification Credits

107 Frequently Asked Questions About Staffing Management, Fiester
(ISBN: 9781586443733)

47 Frequently Asked Questions About the Family and Medical Leave Act, Fiester
(ISBN: 9781586443801)

57 Frequently Asked Questions About Workplace Safety and Security, Fiester
(ISBN: 9781586443610)

97 Frequently Asked Questions About Compensation, Fiester
(ISBN: 9781586443566)

A Manager's Guide to Developing Competencies in HR Staff, Hartman
(ISBN: 9781586444365)

A Necessary Evil: Managing Employee Activity on Facebook, Wright
(ISBN: 9781586443412)

Aligning Human Resources and Business Strategy, Holbeche
(ISBN: 9780750680172)

Applying Critical Evaluation: Making an Impact in Small Business, Currence
(ISBN: 9781586444426)

Becoming the Evidence Based Manager, Latham
(ISBN: 9780891063988)

Being Global: How to Think, Act, and Lead in a Transformed World, Cabrera
(ISBN: 9781422183229)

Black Holes and White Spaces: Reimagining the Future of Work and HR, Boudreau
(ISBN: 9781586444617)

Business Literacy Survival Guide for HR Professionals, Garey
(ISBN: 9781586442057)

Business-Focused HR: 11 Processes to Drive Results, Mondore
(ISBN: 9781586442040)

Calculating Success, Hoffman
(ISBN: 9781422166390)

California Employment Law, Revised and Updated, McDonald
(ISBN: 9781586444815)

Collaborate: The Art of We, Sanker
(ISBN: 9781118114728)

Deep Dive: Proven Method for Building Strategy, Horwath
(ISBN: 9781929774821)

Defining HR Success: 9 Critical Competencies for HR Professionals, Alonso
(ISBN: 9781586443825)

Destination Innovation: HR's Role in Charting the Course, Buhler
(ISBN: 9781586443832)

Developing Business Acumen, Currence
(ISBN: 9781586444143)

Developing Proficiency in HR: 7 Self-Directed Activities for HR Professionals, Cohen
(ISBN: 9781586444167)

Digital HR: A Guide to Technology- Enabled Human Resources, Waddill
(ISBN: 9781586445423)

Diverse Teams at Work: Capitalizing on the Power of Diversity, Gardenswartz
(ISBN: 9781586440367)

Effective Human Resource Management: A Global Analysis, Lawler
(ISBN: 9780804776875)

Emotional Intelligence 2.0, Bradberry
(ISBN: 9780974320625)

Financial Analysis for HR Managers, Director
(ISBN: 9780133925425)

From Hello to Goodbye, 2e, Walters
(ISBN: 9781586444471)

From We Will to at Will: A Handbook for Veteran Hiring, Constantine
(ISBN: 9781586445072)

Give Your Company a Fighting Chance, Danaher
(ISBN: 9781586443658)

Go Beyond the Job Description, Lesko
(ISBN: 9781586445171)

Good People, Bad Managers: How Work Culture Corrupts Good Intentions, Culbert
(ISBN: 9780190652395)

Got a Minute? The 9 Lessons Every HR Professional Must Learn to Be Successful, Dwyer
(ISBN: 9781586441982)

Got a Solution? HR Approaches to 5 Common and Persistent Business Problems, Dwyer
(ISBN: 9781586443665)

Handbook for Strategic HR: Best Practices in Organization Development, Vogelsang
(ISBN: 9780814432495)

Hidden Drivers of Success: Leveraging Employee Insights for Strategic Advantage, Schiemann
(ISBN: 9781586443337)

HR at Your Service: Lessons from Benchmark Service Organizations, Latham
(ISBN: 9781586442477)

HR on Purpose: Developing Deliberate People Passion, Browne
(ISBN: 9781586444259)

HR Transformation: Building Human Resources from the Inside Out, Ulrich
(ISBN: 9780071638708)

HR's Greatest Challenge: Driving the C-Suite to Improve Employee Engagement …, Finnegan
(ISBN: 9781586443795)

Humanity Works: Merging Technologies and People for the Workforce of the Future, Levit
(ISBN: 9780749483456)

Investing in People: Financial Impact of Human Resource Initiatives, 2e, Boudreau
(ISBN: 9780132394116)

Investing in What Matters: Linking Employees to Business Outcomes, Mondore
(ISBN: 9781586441371)

Leadership from the Mission Control Room to the Boardroom, Hill
(ISBN: 9780998634319)

Leading an HR Transformation, Anderson
(ISBN: 9781586444860)

Leading the Unleadable, Willett
(ISBN: 9780814437605)

Leading with Dignity, Hicks
  (ISBN: 9780300229639)

*Lean HR: Introducing Process Excellence to
  Your Practice*, Lay
  (ISBN: 9781481914208)

*Linkage Inc.'s Best Practices for Succession
  Planning: Case Studies, Research,
  Models, Tools*, Sobol
  (ISBN: 9780787985790)

Looking to Hire an HR Leader, Hartman
  (ISBN: 9781586443672)

*Manager 3.0: A Millennial's Guide to
  Rewriting the Rules of Management*,
  Karsh
  (ISBN: 9780814432891)

*Manager Onboarding: 5 Steps for Setting New
  Leaders Up for Success*, Lauby
  (ISBN: 9781586444075)

Manager's Guide to Employee Engagement,
  Carbonara
  (ISBN: 9780071799508)

Managing Employee Turnover, Allen
  (ISBN: 9781606493403)

Managing the Global Workforce, Caligiuri
  (ISBN: 9781405107327)

*Managing the Mobile Workforce: Leading,
  Building, and Sustaining Virtual Teams*,
  Clemons
  (ISBN: 9780071742207)

*Managing the Older Worker: How to Prepare
  for the New Organizational Order*,
  Cappelli
  (ISBN: 9781422131657)

Mastering Consultation as an HR Practitioner,
  Currence
  (ISBN: 9781586445027)

*Measuring ROI in Employee Relations and
  Compliance*, Phillips
  (ISBN: 9781586443597)

*Motivation-Based Interviewing: A
  Revolutionary Approach to Hiring the
  Best*, Quinn
  (ISBN: 9781586445478)

*Multipliers: How the Best Leaders Make
  Everyone Smarter*, Wiseman
  (ISBN: 9780061964398)

*Negotiation at Work: Maximize Your Team's
  Skills with 60 High-Impact Activities*,
  Asherman
  (ISBN: 9780814431900)

*New Power: How Power Works in Our
  Hyperconnected World*, Heimans
  (ISBN: 9780385541114)

*Nine Minutes on Monday: The Quick and
  Easy Way to Go from Manager to
  Leader*, Robbins
  (ISBN: 9780071801980)

*One Life: How Organisations Can Leverage
  Work-Life Integration*, Uhereczky
  (ISBN: 9782874035180)

*One Strategy: Organizing, Planning and
  Decision Making*, Sinofsky
  (ISBN: 9780470560457)

Organizational Design that Sticks, Albrecht
  (ISBN: 9781948699006)

Peer Coaching at Work, Parker
  (ISBN: 9780804797092)

*People Analytics: How Social Sensing
  Technology Will Transform Business*,
  Waber
  (ISBN: 9780133158311)

Perils and Pitfalls of California Employment Law: A Guide for HR Professionals, Effland
(ISBN: 9781586443634)

Point Counterpoint II: New Perspectives on People & Strategy, Vosburgh
(ISBN: 9781586444181)

Point Counterpoint: New Perspectives on People & Strategy, Tavis
(ISBN: 9781586442767)

Practices for Engaging the 21st-Century Workforce, Castellano
(ISBN: 9780133086379)

Predicting Business Success: Using Smarter Analytics to Drive Results, Mondore
(ISBN: 9781586445379)

Preventing Workplace Harassment in a #MeToo World, Dominick
(ISBN: 9781586445539)

Proving the Value of HR: How and Why to Measure ROI, Phillips
(ISBN: 9781586442316)

Reality Based Leadership, Wakeman
(ISBN: 9780470613504)

Reinventing Jobs: A 4-Step Approach for Applying Automation to Work, Jesuthasan
(ISBN: 9781633694071)

Rethinking Retention in Good Times and Bad, Finnegan
(ISBN: 9780891062387)

Social Media Strategies for Professionals and Their Firms, Golden
(ISBN: 9780470633106)

Solving the Compensation Puzzle: Putting Together a Complete Pay and Performance System, Koss
(ISBN: 9781586440923)

StandOut 2.0: Assess Your Strengths, Find Your Edge, Win at Work, Buckingham
(ISBN: 9781633690745)

Stop Bullying at Work, 2e, Daniel
(ISBN: 9781586443856)

Talent, Transformation, and the Triple Bottom Line, Savitz
(ISBN: 9781118140970)

The ACE Advantage: How Smart Companies Unleash Talent for Optimal Performance, Schiemann
(ISBN: 9781586442866)

The Big Book of HR, Mitchell
(ISBN: 9781601631893)

The Circle Blueprint: Decoding the Conscious and Unconscious Factors …, Skeen
(ISBN: 9781119434856)

The Crowdsourced Performance Review, Mosley
(ISBN: 9780071817981)

The Cultural Fit Factor: Creating an Employment Brand That Attracts …, Pellet
(ISBN: 9781586441265)

The Definitive Guide to HR Communication, Davis
(ISBN: 9780137061433)

The Employee Engagement Mindset, Clark
(ISBN: 9780071788298)

The EQ Interview: Finding Employees with High Emotional Intelligence, Lynn
(ISBN: 9780814409411)

The Global Challenge: International Human Resource Management, 2nd ed., Evans
(ISBN: 9780073530376)

The Global M&A Tango, Trompenaars
(ISBN: 9780071761154)

*The Hard Talk Handbook: The Definitive
Guide to Having the Difficult
Conversations …*, Metcalfe (ASIN:
B07J2C8YF5)

The HR Answer Book, 2e, Smith
(ISBN: 9780814417171)

*The HR Career Guide: Great Answers to
Tough Career Questions*, Yate
(ISBN: 9781586444761)

*The HR Insider: How to Land Your Dream Job,
and Keep It!*, Jeshani
(ISBN: 9781717475565)

The Manager's Guide to HR, 2e, Muller
(ISBN: 9780814433027)

The Performance Appraisal Tool Kit, Falcone
(ISBN: 9780814432631)

*The Power of Appreciative Inquiry: A Practical
Guide to Positive Change, 2nd ed.*,
Whitney
(ISBN: 9781605093284)

*The Power of Stay Interviews for Retention and
Engagement*, 2e, Finnegan
(ISBN: 9781586445126)

The Practical Guide to HR Analytics, Waters
(ISBN: 9781586445324)

The Recruiter's Handbook, Lauby
(ISBN: 9781586444655)

*The SHRM Essential Guide to Employment
Law*, Fleischer
(ISBN: 9781586444709)

*The Square and the Triangle: The Power of
Integrating Relationships …*, Stevens
(ISBN: 9781612061474)

*The Talent Fix: A Leader's Guide to Recruiting
Great Talent*, Sackett
(ISBN: 9781586445225)

*Thinking in Bets: Making Smarter Decisions
When You Don't Have All the Facts*,
Duke
(ISBN: 9780735216358)

*Thrive By Design: The Neuroscience That
Drives High-Performance Cultures*,
Rheem
(ISBN: 9781946633064)

Touching People's Lives: Leaders' Sorrow or Joy,
Losey
(ISBN: 9781586444310)

Transformational Diversity, Citkin
(ISBN: 9781586442309)

*Transformative HR: How Great Companies
Use Evidence-Based Change …*,
Boudreau
(ISBN: 9781118036044)

*Type R: Transformative Resilience for Thriving
in a Turbulent World*, Marston
(ISBN: 9781610398060)

*Up, Down, and Sideways: High-Impact Verbal
Communication for HR Professionals*,
Buhler
(ISBN: 9781586443375)

*View from the Top: Leveraging Human and
Organization Capital to Create Value*,
Wright
(ISBN: 9781586444006)

*WE: Men, Women, and the Decisive Formula
for Winning at Work*, Anderson
(ISBN: 9781119524694)

*Weathering Storms: Human Resources in
Difficult Times*, SHRM
(ISBN: 9781586441340)

*What If? Short Stories to Spark Diversity
Dialogue*, Robbins
(ISBN: 9780891062752)

What Is Global Leadership? 10 Key Behaviors
that Define Great Global Leaders,
Gundling
(ISBN: 9781904838234)

Winning the War for Talent in Emerging
Markets: Why Women are the Solution,
Hewlett
(ISBN: 9781422160602)

Work Rules!: Insights from Inside Google That
Will Transform How You Live and Lead,
Bock
(ISBN: 9781455554799)